PELICAN BOOKS

SELF AND OTHERS

Dr R. D. Laing was born in Glasgow and graduated from the university there. He has worked as an army psychiatrist and with various hospitals and clinics, including the Tavistock Institute of Human Relations, where he did research into families from 1961 to 1967. His research is particularly concerned with schizophrenia, families, and varieties of experience including mind-expanding drugs. His other books are *Knots*, *Reason and Violence* (with David Cooper), *Interpersonal Perception* (with H. Phillipson and A. R. Lee), *Sanity, Madness and the Family* (with A. Esterson), *The Divided Self*, *The Politics of Experience* and *The Bird of Paradise*.

SELF
AND OTHERS

R. D. LAING

PENGUIN BOOKS

Penguin Books Ltd, Harmondsworth, Middlesex, England
Penguin Books Inc., 7110 Ambassador Road, Baltimore, Maryland 21207, U.S.A.
Penguin Books Australia Ltd, Ringwood, Victoria, Australia

—

First published in Great Britain by Tavistock Publications 1961
Second edition 1969
First published in the U.S.A. by Pantheon Books Inc. 1969
Published in Pelican Books 1971

—

—

Made and printed in Great Britain by
C. Nicholls & Company Ltd
Set in Monotype Garamond

Contents

Preface to the Second Edition

THIS book has been extensively revised, without being changed in any fundamental way. It remains an attempt to weave experience and behaviour into a consistent theory, since they are so woven in real life. The theoretical tendency to split the two still continues since this book was written. I would like to regard it as standing with those comparatively few efforts made in recent years to understand relations between persons in personal terms.

I hope the erudite reader will not be confused by my particularly parochial use of the term phantasy. Another study would be necessary to review the different usages of this term in Western thought, and even the different ways it is employed within psychoanalysis itself. Freud's use of the concept of unconscious phantasy has been critically reviewed by Laplanche and Pontalis (1964, 1968).

Some of the puzzles posed by the concept of unconscious phantasy may be resolved by bringing into play the theory of mapping. I have recently sketched how this may be done (Laing, 1969).

Briefly, if I project an element x from set A on to an element y of set B, and if we call the operation of projection or mapping ø, then y is called the image of x under ø. The operation ø is a function whereby y acquires the ø-value of x. Johnny is the image of his grandfather. A set of relations may be mapped on to another set of relations, and elements of one set may be mapped on to themselves. This is not the place to develop this, but it is perhaps appropriate merely to suggest that this formula seems to me to clarify the double usage of phantasy, as in the expressions: the 'contents' of phantasy, and phantasy as a 'function'. As a function, phantasy can be regarded as an operation of mapping, from any domain of experience to any range of experience. It seems to me even possible to conceive of mapping desires (instincts), not experienced *in* themselves, as it were, on to experience, such that the range of experience so mapped acquires a ø (phantasy)-value, and

7

to conceive that a person may not himself recognize that this range of his experience has acquired such a ø-value, usually called the unconscious 'content' of phantasy.

R.D.L.

London, May 1969

Preface to the First Edition

I SHALL try to depict persons within a social system or 'nexus' of persons, in order to try to understand some of the ways in which each affects each person's experience of himself and of how interaction takes form. Each contributes to the other's fulfilment or destruction.

This book is part of the outcome of research on interactional processes, particularly in marriages and families, with particular but not exclusive references to psychosis, based on the Tavistock Institute of Human Relations and the Tavistock Clinic. I wish to thank these organizations for facilitating the work in all its aspects.

The latter stages in the preparation of the manuscript were greatly helped by a Fellowship from the Foundations Fund for Research in Psychiatry, which I gratefully acknowledge.

The book owes a great deal to many sources which are, for the most part, little discussed in the text itself – psychoanalysis, particularly the work of Fairbairn, Melanie Klein, Bion, Winnicott, Rycroft, Erikson, Marion Milner; analytical psychology; and American research in communication, person perception, and family process.

Over the past two years much of this book has been discussed by colleagues and friends. I should like to thank in particular Dr Karl Abenheimer, Mr J. A. Ambrose, Dr John Bowlby, Dr David Cooper, Dr A. Esterson, Dr Marie Jahoda, Dr P. E. S. Lomas, Dr E. P. Michell, Mrs Marion Milner, Professor J. Romano, Dr Charles Rycroft, Dr Dennis Scott, Dr Paul Senft, Dr J. D. Sutherland, Dr D. W. Winnicott; also my research colleagues, Dr A. Russell Lee and Mr Herbert Phillipson. Dr Lee is completing a monograph on 'Schizophrenia and the Family Nexus'.

R. D. LAING

London, June 1961

Acknowledgements

THANKS are due to the authors and to the Editor of *Behavioral Science* for permission to quote from 'Toward a Theory of Schizophrenia' by G. Bateson, D. D. Jackson, J. Haley, and J. Weakland; to the Editor of the *British Journal of Medical Psychology* in respect of 'The Effort to Drive the other Person Crazy – an Element in the Etiology and Psychotherapy of Schizophrenia' by H. F. Searles; to Professor M. Buber, George Allen & Unwin, and the Editors of the *Hibbert Journal* and *Psychiatry* in respect of 'Distance and Relation' and 'Elements of the Interhuman Contact'; to Jean Genet in respect of *The Balcony*, translated by Bernard Frechtman; to The Harvill Press in respect of *The Double: A Poem of St Petersburg* by F. Dostoyevsky; to the Hogarth Press in respect of *Trends in Psycho-Analysis* by M. Brierley; to Librairie Gallimard in respect of *Saint Genet. Comédien et Martyr* by Jean-Paul Sartre (*tous droits réservés*); to The Melanie Klein Trust in respect of 'The Nature and Function of Phantasy' by Susan Isaacs from *Developments in Psycho-Analysis*, edited by J. Rivière; to Methuen & Co. in respect of *Being and Nothingness* by Jean-Paul Sartre; to The Olympia Press in respect of *Notre Dame des Fleurs* by Jean Genet; to Penguin Books in respect of *Crime and Punishment* by F. Dostoyevsky; to The Psychoanalytic Quarterly Inc. in respect of *Thalassa: A Theory of Genitality* by S. Ferenczi.

The way out is via the door. Why is it that no one will use this method?

CONFUCIUS

Part One

Modes of Interpersonal Experience

CHAPTER I

Phantasy and Experience

WE talk, in a rough and ready way, of acts and experiences 'in memory', 'in dreams', 'in imagination', and 'in reality'. Some psychoanalysts propose that we can also talk about experiences 'in' 'unconscious phantasy'. But is unconscious phantasy a mode or a type of experience? If it is, it is with a difference. If not, what is it, if not a figment of imagination?

The psychoanalytic thesis can be stated thus: it is not *possible* to prove the existence of unconscious phantasy to the person who is immersed in it. Unconscious phantasy can be known to be phantasy only after the person's own emergence from it. This way of putting it is riddled with difficulties, and so is every other way. The situation is not assisted by the fact that the concept of unconscious phantasy has received very little scrutiny from an existential and phenomenological perspective. And yet no comprehensive account of human relations can ignore it.

A paper[1] by Susan Isaacs (1952) on 'The nature and function of Phantasy' provides a convenient starting-point. I choose to begin with this version of the psychoanalytic theory of phantasy because it remains an influential study that has not been superseded and because Isaacs seems to regard phantasy as, among other things, *a mode of experience*.

1. In particular, this paper has been generally accepted by the Klein group in London as a fundamental statement of their position. It has been attacked by Glover (1945).

I

Isaacs states that she is 'mostly concerned with the definition of "phantasy"; that is to say, with describing the *series of facts* which the use of the term helps us to identify, to organize and to relate to other significant facts' (p. 67).

She summarizes her argument as follows:

1. The concept of phantasy has gradually widened in psycho-analytic thought. It now requires clarification and explicit expansion in order to integrate all the relevant facts.
2. On the views here developed:
   (a) Phantasies are the primary content of unconscious mental processes.
   (b) Unconscious phantasies are primarily about bodies, and represent instinctual aims towards objects.
   (c) These phantasies are, in the first instance, the psychic representatives of libidinal and destructive instincts. Early in development they also become elaborated into defences as well as wish-fulfilments and anxiety contents.
   (d) Freud's postulated 'hallucinatory wish-fulfilment' and his 'primary identification', 'introjection', and 'projection' are the basis of the phantasy life.
   (e) Through external experience, phantasies become elaborated and capable of expression, but they do not depend upon such experience for their existence.
   (f) Phantasies are not dependent upon words, although they may under certain conditions be capable of expression in words.
   (g) The earliest phantasies are experienced as sensations: later they take the form of plastic images and dramatic representations.
   (h) Phantasies have both psychic and bodily effects, e.g. in conversion symptoms, bodily qualities, character and personality, neurotic symptoms, inhibitions and sublimations.
   (i) Unconscious phantasies form the operative link between instincts and mechanism. When studied in detail, every

variety of ego-mechanism can be seen to arise from specific sorts of phantasy, which in the last resort have their origin in instinctual impulses. 'The ego is a differentiated part of the id.' A 'mechanism' is an abstract general term describing certain mental processes which are experienced by the subject as unconscious phantasies.

(j) Adaptation to reality and reality-thinking require the support of concurrent unconscious phantasies. Observation of the ways in which knowledge of the external world develops shows how the child's phantasy contributes to his learning.

(k) Unconscious phantasies exert a continuous influence throughout life, both in normal and neurotic people, the differences lying in the specific character of the dominant phantasies, the desire or anxiety associated with them and their interplay with each other and with external reality (pp. 111–12).

The term phantasy is intended to point to a series of facts. What is the *domain* of this series of facts? Are they facts *of* experience? Of my experience? Of your experience? Of my experience of you, but not of *your* experience of yourself? Are they facts, not *of* my experience, but inferred from facts of my experience? By me about me? By me about you? Does their domain lie anywhere in the experience of self and other, or outside all experience, albeit inferred from it? Phantasies are experienced as dramatic representations. What does this mean? Can dramatic representations be experienced as phantasy? Whose, and by whom?

Isaacs's paper is mainly concerned with inferences by *self* about *other*. In my experience, self does not experience the experience of other directly. The facts about other available to self are actions of other experienced by self.

From the perspective of self seeing other, Isaacs infers from her experience of the other's actions certain things about the other's experience.

An adult infers what a baby experiences. The baby does not tell us. The adult infers from the baby's behaviour that the baby's experience of a situation common to the adult and the baby is the same as or different from the adult's experience of the 'same' situation.

Isaacs states: 'Our views about phantasy in these earliest years are based wholly upon inference, but then this is true at any age. Unconscious phantasies are always inferred, not observed as such; the technique of psychoanalysis as a whole is largely based upon inferred knowledge' (p. 69).

To be consistent, we appear to have no option but to maintain that self's knowledge of other's experience, of any kind, conscious or unconscious, is based at any age of self or other entirely upon inference, as Isaacs states firmly in the second sentence above about unconscious phantasy. Since to Isaacs phantasies are 'inner', 'mental' events, only one's own phantasies are *directly* available to self. They *can only* be inferred by the other. The idea that 'the mind', 'the unconscious', or 'phantasy' is located inside a person and, *in that sense*, is inaccessible to the other, has far-reaching effects on the whole of psychoanalytic theory and method.

Isaacs, in referring not simply to imagination, daydreams, or reveries, but to 'unconscious phantasy', is making two types of inference from her position as the own person, namely: she is inferring something about the other's experience, *and* she is inferring that this is something of which the other is unaware. This seems to mean that there is a whole *type* of experience, as well as specific 'content' *of* experience, of which the other who 'has' the imputed experience knows, or may know, nothing. From her premises, corroboration of her self's inferences by explicit testimony from the other is not necessary to confirm these particular inferences.

When self is the analyst and the other the analysand, the own person states:

The personality, the attitudes and intentions, even the external characteristics and the sex of the analyst, *as seen and felt in the patient's mind,* change from day to day (even from moment to moment), according to changes in the inner life of the patient (whether these are brought about by the analyst's comments or by outside happenings). That is to say, *the patient's relation to his analyst is almost entirely one of unconscious phantasy* (p. 78).

The own person infers from the other's behaviour that the other's behaviour has a 'meaning' to which the other is blind and, in that sense, the other cannot 'see' or 'realize' what his (the other's) actions are implying.

The analyst then says: 'The patient is dominated by an "unconscious" phantasy.'

Let us distinguish two usages of 'unconscious'. First, the term 'unconscious' may refer to dynamic structures, functions, mechanisms, processes that are meant to explain a person's actions or experiences. Such structures, functions, mechanisms, or processes are outside experience but are used to 'explain' experience, whether called conscious or unconscious. These concepts lie outside experience, but start from inferences about experience. If these inferences are incorrect, everything built upon them is completely wrong.

In the second place, 'unconscious' may signify that the user of the term is claiming that he or the other is unaware of part of his own experience, despite the apparent absurdity of this claim.

We may ask: what is the experiential status of 'unconscious phantasy' as Isaacs uses this term? Isaacs, time and again, states that unconscious phantasy is an experience:

A mechanism is an abstract general term describing certain mental processes which are *experienced by the subject as unconscious phantasies* (p. 112, italics my own).

And:

Phantasy is (in the first instance) the mental corollary, the psychic representative, of instinct. There is no impulse, no instinctual urge or response *which is not experienced as unconscious phantasy* (p. 83, italics my own).

On the basis of those principles of observation and interpretation which have already been described and are well established by psycho-analytic work, we are able to conclude that when the child shows his desire for his mother's breast, he *experiences* this desire as a specific phantasy – 'I want to suck the nipple'. If desire is very intense (perhaps on account of anxiety), he is likely to feel: 'I want to eat her all up' (p. 84, italics original).

For Isaacs, unconscious phantasy is a way of experiencing our desires which plays a part in our personal relations throughout life.

II

Is it a contradiction in terms to speak of 'unconscious experience'? A person's experience comprises anything that 'he' or 'any part of him' is aware of, whether 'he' or every part of him is aware of every level of his awareness or not. His experiences are inner or outer; of his own body or of other person's bodies; real or unreal; private or shared. The psychoanalytical contention is that our desires present themselves to us in our experience, but we may not recognize them. This is one sense in which we are unconscious of our experience. We misconstrue it.

But even if we can find a formula to avoid using 'unconscious' to qualify experience directly, there are issues in Isaacs's paper that present what seem to be intractable difficulties. They run through the whole of Isaacs's presentation, and through psychoanalytic theory in general. They are crystallized in the following passage:

When contrasted with external and bodily realities, the phantasy, like other mental activities, is a figment, since it cannot be touched or handled or seen; yet it is real in the experience of the subject. It is a true mental function and it has real effects, not only in the inner world of the mind but also in the external world of the subject's bodily development and behaviour, and hence of other people's minds and bodies (p. 99).

Phantasy is 'real in the experience of the subject'. It is also 'a figment, *since* it cannot be touched or handled or seen'. The term denotes both 'real' experiences of which the subject is unconscious, and a mental function which has 'real' effects. These real *effects* are the real experiences. Phantasy appears now to be the *cause* of itself, as an effect, and the effect of itself, as a cause. It may be we are touching upon a critical insight that is obscured by a tangle into which we have been led by some of our theoretical distinctions.

One source of confusion is the particular dichotomous schema in which the whole theory is cast. This particular schema entails the distinction between 'the inner world of the mind', on the one hand, and 'the external world of the subject's bodily development and behaviour, and hence of other people's minds and bodies', on the other.

This contradistinction generates, in Isaacs's paper and in many psychoanalytic works, two opposed clusters of terms, namely:

inner	in contrast to	*outer*
mental	in contrast to	*physical*
mental activity	in contrast to	*external and bodily realities*
figment	in contrast to	*what can be touched, handled, seen*
psychical reality	in contrast to	*physical reality*

the inner world of the mind	in contrast to	*the external world of the subject's bodily development, and hence of other people's minds and bodies*
mind	in contrast to	*body*

In terms of this set of distinctions, we have to suppose that phantasy begins on the left as an inner mental activity, etc., and crosses over somehow to the right. Despite the peculiar position we are led to, we have to suppose it comes to be *experienced* only on the right. For we are told that it is experienced in terms of external and bodily reality, both as to one's own body and as to the bodies of others.

Terms like conversion, a shift from mind to body; projection, a shift from inner to outer; introjection, a shift from outer to inner, are caught and entangled by this theoretical split. Instead of describing facts of experience, they are used to explain artifacts of the theory. The dual series, still less these transitions, does not belong to the series of facts Isaacs sets out to describe. A person may experience himself in terms of this set of distinctions. He 'feels' his 'mind' contains 'contents', he testifies that his 'body' is 'outside' his 'mind'. Strange though this may sound, we may suppose that he is not a liar and is choosing his words carefully. However, it is quite another matter to take such a form of self-division as one's theoretical starting-point.

Phantasy can also be *imagined* to go on 'in' the 'mind'. One may ask why it should be so imagined, without undertaking to work out the imaginary problem itself.

If one does not adopt, or if one gives up, this particular dichotomy of inner–mental and external–physical, other problems come into view. These are not *the same* problems dressed in other words. The true problem at the moment is to allow the problems to arise. They can do so only when the phenomena are no longer masked by false problems.

III

Metapsychology must begin from somebody's experience, but it is seldom clear whose experience or what experience.

Psychoanalysts frequently use the term 'reality' for what makes experience valid. But it is used in all sorts of ways, and may refer, for instance, (i) to that which gives rise to experience; (ii) to a particular 'quality' that some experiences have and others lack; and, quite coarsely, (iii) to whatever 'common sense' or the analyst takes to be the case. Reality itself is put into such slots as 'psychic' reality, 'physical' reality, 'internal' reality and 'external' reality, 'subjective' reality and 'objective' reality.

It is useful to distinguish *quality* from *mode* of experience. Dreaming is a mode of experience that the waking person distinguishes from waking perception by various criteria. Dreaming, imagination, and waking perception are different modes of experience. 'Reality' in the second sense above, may be a quality attached at times to any of these modalities.

'Internal' and 'external' may be used to refer to 'reality' in the first sense. 'Inner reality' may be said to give rise to outer experience or to inner experience, and vice versa. In either case the 'reality' in the second sense, which generates the experience, may be regarded as 'internal' or 'external' to the presumed boundary of self or other. 'Internal' is sometimes a synonym for 'psychic' or 'subjective' in contrast to 'external', 'physical', or 'objective'. 'Internal' and 'external' may also be used to discriminate between dreams and waking life, or 'imaginary' and 'real' events, where the distinction is between modes of experience.

'Mind' is frequently used as a reality outside experience from which experience comes. Thus Jack admits that Jill has peculiar bodily feelings, but imputes their origin to 'the mind' of Jill. They are 'psychogenic' and Jill is 'hysterical'. If the body is classified, as by Isaacs, as part of 'external reality' – 'external', that is, to 'the mind' – Jack evokes 'conversion' to 'explain' how an 'event' 'in' the 'mind' of Jill is experienced by Jill not 'in' her 'mind' but 'in' her 'body', that is, 'in' 'external' or 'physical' 'reality'.

When employed in this way, concepts like conversion, projection, or introjection, do not *describe* what is actually going on in anyone's experience. As 'mechanisms' intended as 'explanations' of experience, it is impossible to tell what experiences they are intended to 'explain'. As mechanisms to provide a shuttle service between inner and outer realities, they ply between the distinctions we examined above, of psychical and physical, inner and outer, mind and body. Used in this way, they describe nothing, explain nothing, and are themselves inexplicable. A bodily experience is called a 'mental event', but 'external to the mind'. To explain itself, the theory spirals from non-phenomenological postulates masquerading as experiential attributions to postulates devised to 'explain' how what is 'in' the 'mind' is experienced as 'outside' 'the mind' 'in' the 'body'.

Jack attributes to Jill experiences *and* attributes to Jill unconsciousness of them. Jill agrees that she is not aware of them. In *meta*psychology, Jack now tries to 'explain' not merely his construction of data directly available to him, but very often his own explanations of what never were data. When Jack infers that Jill 'has' experiences, past or present, of which she is unconscious, he is taking a portentous step, beyond his own experience of Jill *and* beyond Jill's experience of herself or of him. Jack has no guarantee that he is not stepping beyond *his* and Jill's experience, straight through the looking-glass back into his own projections.

My impression is that most adult Europeans and North

Americans would subscribe to the following: the other person's experience is not directly experienced by self. For the present it does not matter whether this is necessarily so, is so elsewhere on the planet, or has always been the case. But if we agree that you do not experience my experience, we agree that we rely on our communications to give us our clues as to how or what we are thinking, feeling, imagining, dreaming, and so forth. Things are going to be difficult if you tell me that I am *experiencing* something which I am not experiencing. If that is what I think you mean by unconscious experience.

As far as I know, there is no comparable practical and theoretical set of problems in natural science. Natural scientists do not try to infer how *anima mundi* experiences their interventions into natural process. But even natural scientists are aware that people experience one another. Only some psychologists seem to be unaware of this.

Attribution to the other of experience of which the other is unconscious is something else again. It is premature to speak of an already existent systematic method of investigating the field of inter-experience, let alone the phenomenology *of* such a method.

We attribute motives, agency, intention, and experiences to one another all the time. The investigation of who attributes what to whom, when, why, and how is a science in itself. In addition to this whole set of problems that could absorb many lifetimes without exhausting them, there are the questions directed to the logic of valid inference in such a prospective science of person-to-person relations.

The science of personal relations is not assisted by the fact that only a few psychologists are concerned to discover valid personal ways in which persons, and relations between persons, can be studied by persons. Many pscyhologists feel that if psychology is not a branch of natural science it is not a science at all.

On the contrary. If I want to get to know you, it is unlikely that I shall if I proceed as though I were studying nebulae or rats. You will not be inclined to disclose yourself to me. Whatever else I may be studying, I shall not be studying *you* if I do not know you. If you are adept at self-concealment, you may be justifiably confident that I shall not learn much about you by scrutinizing your behaviour alone. If one says that all one is interested in is the study of behaviour 'pure and simple', then one is not studying persons. But at present many psychologists hold in effect that it is scientifically impossible to do so.

It is impossible to derive the basic logic of a science of persons from the logic of non-personal sciences. No branch of natural science requires to make the peculiar type of inferences that are required in a science of persons.

One person investigating the experience of another can be directly aware only of his own experience of the other. He cannot have direct awareness of the other's experience of the 'same' world. He cannot see through the other's eyes and cannot hear through the other's ears. The only true voyage, Proust once remarked, would be not to travel through a hundred different lands with the same pair of eyes, but to see the same land through a hundred different pairs of eyes. All one 'feels', 'senses', 'intuits', etc. of the other entails inference from one's own experience of the other to the other's experience of one's self. This presupposes that the other's actions are in some way a function of the other's experience, as I know mine to be. Only on the basis of this presupposition, however qualified it may be, can one hazard inferences about the other's experience from one's perspective of the other's actions.

The inferences that one makes about the other's experience from one's direct and immediate perceptions of the other person's actions are one class of acts of attribution.[2] No other science can supply adequate criteria for the validity of such personal attributions.

Too many, not all, psychoanalysts plunge right in and out of a revolving door at the threshold of phenomenology, and a second lunge carries others right away from science of any kind. Beyond the mere attribution of agency, motive, intention, experiences that the patient disclaims, there is an extraordinary exfoliation of forces, energies, dynamics, economics, processes, structures to explain the 'unconscious'. Psychoanalytic concepts of this doubly chimerical order include concepts of mental structures, economics, dynamisms, death and life instincts, internal objects,[3] etc. They are postulated as principles of regularity, governing or underlying forces, governing or underlying experience that Jack thinks Jill has, but does not know she has, as inferred by Jack from Jack's experience of Jill's behaviour. In the meantime, what *is* Jack's experience of Jill, Jill's experience of herself, or Jill's experience of Jack?

The situation is often worse than this because it is often not even clear what is experience and what is not, and what is supposed to explain what. Imagined experiences are explained by processes that are themselves doubly imaginary.

Jill may or may not agree that she experiences herself, Jack, or the situation, or that she is acting, in the ways attributed to her by him. But Jack is way ahead of her. His inferences are often not even about how Jill sees herself, how Jill sees Jack, or how Jill sees the situation she shares with Jack.

2. Following the usage of person perception psychology; see especially Heider (1958).

3. 'Internal object' is used sometimes phenomenologically, sometimes metapsychologically. For a lucid psychoanalytic statement on this ambiguity, see Strachey (1941).

Yet the whole of psychoanalytic theory rests upon the validity of such inferences; if they are wrong, everything built upon them loses its *raison d'être*. I am not suggesting that psychoanalysis *ends* at this level of inference. I am saying that unless it *begins* from there it will never get started at all.

I have not used the term unconscious experience, because I cannot resolve satisfactorily in my mind the contradiction between the two words. I am aware that this difficulty could possibly be resolved by a careful definition of unconscious and experience, but in resolving the difficulty one seems to lose the baby with the bathwater.

Experience, as I want to exploy the term, does not exist without an experiencer. An experiencer does not exist without experience. However, one human being experiences different things in different ways, at different times, and even at the same time.

At *one* time, Peter is with Paul

$$
\begin{array}{c}
\text{Imagines} \\
\nearrow \\
\text{Peter} \longrightarrow \text{hears} \\
\swarrow \qquad\qquad \text{sees} \\
\text{remembers} \qquad \text{and understands Paul talking to him}
\end{array}
$$

let us call Peter imagining p_i
Peter remembering p_m
Peter perceiving p_p

Peter, at the one time, includes p_i, p_m, p_p.

p_i experiences in imagination
p_m experiences in memory
p_p experiences in perception

Imagination, memory, perception are three modes of experience.

All of Peter is not in communication with Paul.

The part of Peter in communication with Paul may not know even of the existence of p_i and p_m. The part of Peter in communication with Paul may know that 'he', p_i, is imagining something, but be unable to say what it is.

In that case, I would be prepared to say, speaking in a rough and ready way, that Peter is split. He is unconscious of his imagination, at that moment. The part of Peter in communication with Paul is unconscious of what is going on in his imagination. Peter is *not communicating with himself very well*.

One hour later, Peter is with Jill.

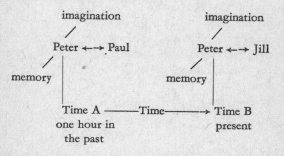

The part of Peter that is in communication with Jill can remember that when he was so bored with that awful conversation with Paul, her husband, he was imagining what it would be like to make love to her when he could get away from Paul, and was remembering the last time they did so. He can even remember, when he is with Jill, that his mind seems to go a blank when he is with Paul; but now, with Jill, curiously enough he cannot remember what Paul was saying to him.

Some people seem to have 'a way with them', so that somehow or other in their presence others seem able to remember what they so often forget, and seem to know, while imagining, *that* they are imagining, and *what* they are imagining.

Once a split is dissolved in the present, memory is *always* opened to some extent. For in becoming aware of a present memory one remembers, let us say, the last time one was thinking of that, which was when one was imagining this, when one was with so and so, and so on. But the difficulty is that as some doors open, others close.

The 'unconscious' is what we do not communicate, to ourselves or to one another. We may convey something to another, without communicating it to ourselves. Something about Peter is evident to Paul that is not evident to Peter. This is *one* sense of the phrase, 'Peter is unconscious of ...'

CHAPTER 2

Phantasy and Communication

WE are in the habit of distinguishing experience in different ways. Some of the most common distinctions are: inner and outer, real and unreal, full and empty, meaningful, futile, private, public, shared. Terms make distinctions in time between past and present, here and now, then and there. Most of us regard part of all we experience at any time and place as 'me' and the rest as 'not-me'. We also categorize the type of experience by modality: namely, memory, imagination, dreaming, waking perception, and so on.

In the above paragraph and the rest of the chapter I intend only to allude to some ways in which such terms are used, and to amplify the discussion of the psychoanalytic concept of 'phantasy' and 'unconscious experience'.

The 'I's in the following paragraphs are hypothetical selves to some of which some of us may subscribe.

I think of me being inside my body and at the same time the inside of my body being somehow 'inside' my private space. If someone comes into my room unasked he does not intrude upon me to the same extent as if he were to enter my body without permission. However since I am inside my body, my body is also outside me in some peculiar sense.

Bodily feelings are usually felt to be real. Physical pain is very real. People seldom feel any feeling they take to be physical is unreal, although some people are given to calling a pain I feel '*your* imagination', if *they* think I have insufficient reasons to feel it. Some people do not feel their bodies to be real and this is grounds *per se* in our culture to consider them as mentally ill.

I have also met people who are prepared to call 'real' pain they themselves feel 'imagination', though this seems to be rare.

Human bodies have a threefold position in personal space, since all other objects are external to *all* men. We usually suppose that the other's body is shareable with him in some respects, a public event shareable by all *except* him (as an object outside everyone else), and, third, private to him.

Our culture, while allowing certain marginal licence, comes down very sharply on people who do not draw the inner/outer, real/unreal, me/not-me, private/public lines where it is thought to be healthy, right, and normal to do so.

A hallucinated voice may be taken to be inside me or outside me; real or unreal; private, in that I may not think anyone else can hear it, or public, if I think others can. Unreal is not synonymous with imaginary. I am supposed to keep my imagination inside myself. Others will usually feel that there is something the matter with me if I think that what I 'imagine' is going on outside my 'mind', *especially* if I call it my imagination and imagine that others do not imagine the same. If two or more persons share such experiences, they are inclined to suppose them to be real. Those who do *not* share them are inclined to suppose that those who do are suffering from some form of shared psychosis.

I take many bodily feelings to be private. If I have a burn on my arm, I take the pain to be private, the sight to be public. This is not always so. Some people feel that they can actually *feel* another person's pain, or think directly another's thoughts, and may feel that other people can feel their bodily feelings, or actually be thinking their thoughts.

My body, as I experience it, is not only shared or public, but a set of private events: namely, the body-for-self. The body-for-self appears in dreams, imagination, and memory. In whichever of these modalities it occurs it may be experienced as alive or dead, real or unreal, whole or in bits. From the standpoint of the reflexive awareness that is regarded as sane, one's own body-for-self is essentially a private experience, and the body-for-self of the other is essentially inaccessible. In phantasy, however, this is not necessarily so. The absence of consensual validation as a court of arbitration on this issue perhaps facilitates its encroachment by phantasy unrecognized as such.

Since each person experiences any event, however public that event may be, in his own way, experience even of public events can be said therefore to be 'private' in a qualified sense. But it is my impression that most people feel that there is an area of experience which is private in an unqualified sense. It is of the area of unqualified privacy that Gerard Manley Hopkins speaks in the following words:

... my self-being, my consciousness and feeling of myself, that taste of myself, of *I* and *me* above and in all things, which is more distinctive than the taste of ale or alum, more distinctive than the smell of walnutleaf or camphor, and is incommunicable by any means to another man (1953, pp. 147–8).

My self-being, my consciousness and feeling of myself, that taste of myself, of I and me above and in all things, includes my taste of you. I taste you and you taste me. I am your taste and you are mine, but I do not taste your taste of me in your ear. One cannot both be everything and have everything at once.

It is difficult to understand the self-being of *the other*. I cannot experience it directly. I must rely on the other's actions and testimony to infer how he experiences himself. The psychiatrist is immediately involved in this area when he listens to the testimony of his patients. By what token do changes in the way a man experiences his self-being, his being-for-himself, determine his own definition of himself as 'ill', 'physically' or 'psychologically', and what leads one person to decide that the self-being, the being-for-himself of the other, is sick?

The Hopkins of ale and alum, of walnutleaf and camphor, was later to write:

> I am gall, I am heartburn. God's most deep decree
> Bitter would have me taste: my taste was me;
> Bones built in me, flesh filled, blood brimmed the curse.
>   Self yeast of spirit a dull dough sours. I see
> The lost are like this, and their scourge to be
> As I am mine, their sweating selves; but worse.
>
>   *(op. cit., p. 62)*

Thousands of people have come to psychiatrists to be 'cured' of less than this. And after the courses of electric shocks, thousands have felt 'better'.

Hopkins knew that this taste, of ale or of gall, was *him*. To be 'cured' of this is more problematical than any other cure, if the cure is to become estranged from one's self-being, to lose one's very self. The loss of the experience of an area of *unqualified privacy*, by its transformation into a quasi-public realm, is often one of the decisive changes associated with the process of going mad. This is not simply a recasting of the 'loss of ego boundary' theory (Laing, 1960, p. 216). Yet even 'the world', although 'common' to all persons and in that sense 'shareable', is possibly never experienced by two individuals in absolutely the same way. When two men look at a landscape, and one likes it and the other does not, there is already a gulf between them. To one man the landscape may simply be itself, full of its 'is-ness': he feels a delicate sadness, perhaps, at his otherness from it. To the other the 'same' trees and sky and grass are seen as creation: as a veil, revealing through themselves their Creator. For one man there may be little or no sense of connection between himself and nature outside himself; for the same person, on another occasion, there may not even be any essential distinctions between inside, outside, self, and nature.

In so far as we experience the world differently, in a sense we live in different worlds. 'The Universe is full of men going through the same motions in the same surroundings, but carrying within themselves, and projecting around them, universes as mutually remote as the constellations' (Mounier, 1952, p. 5). Yet *the* world – the world around me, the world in which I live, *my* world – is, in the very texture of its mode of being-for-me, not exclusively my world, but your world also, it is around you and him as well, it is a shared world, *one* world, *the* world.

There is no necessary correlation between publicity, real-ness, and shareability. Persons can be most alone in their experience of the most public of spectacles; and most together in the sharing of the most 'real', yet unqualifiedly private of events. Sharing a common experience may be a token of the most genuine bond between two persons, or a token of the most abject bondage. Phantasy may or may not be experienced, by either the one person or the other, as inner or outer, private or public, shareable or unshareable, real or unreal.

It is ironical that often what I take to be most public reality turns out to be what others take to be my most private phantasy. And that which I suppose is my most private 'inner' world turns out to be what I have most in common with other human beings.

A psychoanalyst describes his experience at certain moments in a group when he 'feels he is being manipulated so as to be playing a part, no matter how difficult to recognize, in *somebody else's* phantasy – or he would do if it were not for what in recollection I can only call a temporary loss of insight, a sense of experiencing strong feelings, and at the same time a belief that their existence is quite adequately justified by the objective situation without recourse to recondite explanation of their causation' (Bion, 1955, p. 446, italics my own).

This alienation effect is insidious. We are all prone to be drawn into *social phantasy systems* (Jaques, 1955), with loss of one's 'own' identity in the process, and only in retrospect become aware that this has happened. Bion goes on: 'I believe the ability to shake one's self out of the *numbing feeling of reality* that is a concomitant of this state is the prime requisite of the analyst in the group ... ' (op. cit., p. 446, italics my own).

The loss of one's own perceptions and evaluations, which comes with occupying a *false position* (doubly false in that one does not see that it is false), is only 'realized' retrospectively. A false position is not necessarily totally 'untenable'. I shall consider later some of the difficulties in trying to occupy, or to extricate one's self from, an *untenable* position. The person in a doubly false position feels 'real'; without '*feeling*' numb, he is numbed by this very feeling of 'reality'. To shake one's self out of the *false sense of reality* entails a *derealization* of what one falsely takes to be unreality. Only then is one able to apperceive the social phantasy system in which one is. The *normal* state of affairs is to be so immersed in one's immersion in social phantasy systems that one takes them to be real. Many images have been used to remind us of this condition. We are dead, but think we are alive. We are asleep, but think we are awake. We are dreaming, but take our dreams to be reality. We are the halt, lame, blind, deaf, the sick. But we are doubly unconscious. We are *so* ill that we no longer feel ill, as in many terminal illnesses. We are mad, but have no insight.

The error is not so much of content, as of category. We are aware of the *content* of experience, but are unaware that it is illusion. We see the shadows, but take them for the substance. A closely related error of category is to confuse the *modality* of experience. We are ready to see others fall into such error, but it is quite a different matter when it comes to ourselves.

We can see immediately that any discipline that claims to be 'scientific', as this term is usually employed nowadays, and at the same time centrally concerned with the categorization of experience, and with such matters as the unconscious and 'unconscious phantasy', is in very great and *quite peculiar* difficulties about its own criteria of validation.

One does not expect to have one's own impression that the other is doubly alienated confirmed by direct testimony from the other. If the other could agree with us, *we* would be wrong. One can then easily fall into the position that the other's refusal or inability to see that I am right is *proof* that I am right. I could only be proved partially wrong if he did accept what I say, because then I would have erred in thinking that he was unable to see what I think I can see. One may go on to say: but he does not 'really' get it; pseudo-insight.

'Depersonalization' may not be experienced, by those to whom the psychoanalyst attributes depersonalization, as a loss of any personal attributes. It is necessary always to be clear, when one hears or sees this term employed, whether the term depersonalization refers to a state self imputes to self, or is an attribution made by self to other disjunctive with other's self-attribution.

A person in an alienated false position within a social phantasy system, who begins partially to apperceive his position, may give 'psychotic' expression to his partial apperception of the actual phantasy state of affairs by saying that he is being subjected to poisons concealed in his food, that his brains have been taken from him, that his actions are controlled from outer space, etc. *Such delusions are partially achieved derealization-realizations*.

All groups operate by means of phantasy. The type of *experience* a group gives us is one of the main reasons, if not for some people the *only* reason, for being in a group. What do people want to get from the experience of being *in* a particular set of human collectivities?

The close-knit groups that occur in some families and other groupings are bound together by the need to find pseudo-real experience that can be found only through the modality of phantasy. This means that the family is not experienced as the modality of phantasy but as 'reality'. However, 'reality' in this sense is not a modality, but a quality attachable to any modality.

If a family member has a tenable position within the family phantasy system, his call to leave the system in any sense is likely only to come from outside the phantasy system. We vary in readiness, and in desire, to emerge from the unconscious phantasy systems we take to be our realities. As long as we are in apparently tenable positions, we find every reason *not* to suppose that we are in a false sense of reality or unreality, security or insecurity, identity or lack of identity.

A false social sense of reality entails, among other things, phantasy unrecognized as such. If Paul begins to wake up from the family phantasy system, he can only be classified as mad or bad by the family since to them their phantasy *is* reality, and what is not their phantasy is not real. If he testifies to any experience outside what they take to be real and true, he can *only* be involved in a regrettable tissue of phantasy and falsehood, in telling them that what they know to be real and true is a regrettable tissue of phantasy and falsehood, in telling him that what he knows to be real and true, (namely: God has given him a special mission to reveal that what they take to be real is a regrettable tissue of phantasy and falsehood and to this end he walked naked and unashamed down the High Street and does not care that he is disgracing the family) is a regrettable tissue of phantasy and falsehood, for which he needs therapy.

The usual state of affairs is to be in a tenable position in phantasy systems of a nexus. This is usually called having an 'identity' or 'personality'. We never realize we are in it. We never even dream of extricating ourselves. We tolerate, punish, or treat as harmless, bad, or mad those who try to extricate themselves, and tell us that we should also.

A person may be placed in an untenable position comprising a non-compossible set of positions. When his position, or positions in the social phantasy system become such that he can neither stay in nor leave *his own phantasy*, his position is *untenable*.

What is called a psychotic episode *in* one person, can often be understood as a crisis of a peculiar kind in the *inter-experience* of the nexus, as well as in the behaviour of the nexus (see Laing and Esterson, 1964; Laing, 1967b).

One way that one may try to get out of the family is to get the family inside one's self, so that one can be outside one's own inside and thus be free. But anywhere one goes one has to go elsewhere, so one decides to settle down and have some place to call one's own.

The greater need there is to get out of an untenable position, the less chance there is of doing so. *The more untenable a position is, the more difficult it is to get out of it.* This tautology is worth pondering upon.

By untenable, I mean that it is impossible to leave and impossible to stay.

In an alienated untenable position one does not realize this. Hence it is impossible to get out. As soon as Paul realizes that he is in a box, he can try to get out of it. But since to *them* the box is *the whole world*, to get out of the box is tantamount to stepping off the end of the world, a thing that no one who loves him could sit by and let happen.

To further the understanding of the bond and/or bondage in the inter-experience of persons, we shall have to show how each person affects the others' phantasy so that his phantasy becomes either more conjunctive or disjunctive with their phantasy. As one person's experience of a situation he is in with others comes to be more disjunctive with that of the others in the 'same' situation, his actions become more and more dissonant with the actions of the others. At some point in the developing disjunction of experience and dissonance of action, the minority comes to be judged by the majority as 'different'.

'Reality' moves from relative to absolute. The more the man we think is absolutely wrong thinks he is absolutely right and we are absolutely wrong, the sooner that man has to be destroyed before he destroys himself or us. We do not (of course) mean that we want to destroy him. We want to save him from his terrible delusion that we want to destroy him. Can't he see that all we want to do is to destroy his delusion? His delusion that we want to destroy him. His delusion is the belief that we are trying to stick pins in his eyes. Someone who thinks that people are sticking pins in his eyes may go along to a psychiatrist to have himself leucotomized by pins being stuck in his eyes, because he would rather even believe he was mad than that it might be real.

The quality of reality experienced inside the nexus of phantasy may be enchanting. Outside it is cold, empty, meaningless, unreal. It is not desirable and, thank God, it is not possible to leave.

It is certainly not easy. But to a number of people the phantasy system of the nexus is a lousy hell, not an enchanting spell, and they want out. But it is bad to want out, that shows ingratitude. It is mad to want to walk out, there is an abyss there, there are wild beasts. Besides don't worry, even despite your ingratitude, and your perversity, you can still be grateful to us that we will not *let* you walk out. The doctor will show you that you don't really want to walk out, you are just running away from us backwards because you are frightened of having a knife stuck in your back. You know we wouldn't do that.

The choice in phantasy comes to be to suffocate to death inside, or to risk exposing one's self to whatever terrors there may be outside. But as soon as one goes through a door in a space that is now inside, one is back right inside the inside that one took inside from the outside in order to get outside what one was inside. So as soon as one goes through that door *that way*, one is more *inside* the more one thinks one is outside.

When inside and outside have been flipped so that inside-outside for A is outside-inside for B and *both* think 'absolutely', then we have spiralled into the most extreme inter-experiential disjunction in our culture – psychiatrists, sane: patients, psychotic. The psychiatrist in this case has no doubt about the diagnosis. The patient is psychotic without insight. The patient thinks the psychiatrist is psychotic and without insight. The patient is psychotic and without insight *because* he thinks that psychiatrists are dangerous lunatics who ought to be locked up for their own safety, and if other people are too much under the spell of the thought-police to see that, he is going to do something about it.

The way out is via the door. But within the phantasy of the nexus, to leave is an act of ingratitude, or cruelty, or suicide, or murder. First steps have to be taken still within the phantasy, before it can be apperceived as such. Herein is the risk of defeat and madness.

Some 'psychotics' look on psychoanalysis as a relatively safe place to tell someone what they really think. They are prepared to play at being a patient and even to keep up the charade by *paying* the analyst, providing he does not 'cure' them. They are even prepared to pretend to be cured if it will look bad for him if he is having a run of people who don't seem to be getting better.

Not an unreasonable contract.

CHAPTER 3

Pretence and Elusion

Let us consider this waiter in the café. His movement is quick and forward, a little too precise, a little too rapid. He comes toward the patrons with a step a little too quick. He bends forward a little too eagerly; his voice, his eyes express an interest a little too solicitous for the order of the customer. Finally there he returns, trying to imitate in his walk the inflexible stiffness of some kind of automaton while carrying his tray with the recklessness of a tight-rope-walker by putting it in a perpetually unstable, perpetually broken equilibrium which he perpetually re-establishes by a light movement of the arm and hand. All his behaviour seems to us a game. He applies himself to chaining his movements as if they were mechanisms, the one regulating the other; his gestures and even his voice seem to be mechanisms; he gives himself the quickness and pitiless rapidity of things. He is playing, he is amusing himself. But what is he playing? We need not watch long before we can explain it: he is playing at *being* a waiter in a café.

JEAN-PAUL SARTRE (1957, p. 59)

OUR perception of 'reality' is the perfectly achieved accomplishment of our civilization. To perceive *reality*! When did people stop feeling that what they *perceived* was *unreal*? Perhaps the feeling and the idea that what we perceive is real is very recent in human history.

Sit in a room. Imagine that the room is not real, that one is conjuring it up: $(A \to B)$. Having pretended this point almost to convincing oneself that the room is imaginary, start to pretend that it is real and not imaginary after all: $(B \to A_1)$. End up by pretending that the room is real, not perceiving it as real.

44

Elusion is a relation in which one pretends oneself away from one's original self; then pretends oneself back from this pretence so as to appear to have arrived back at the starting-point. A double pretence simulates no pretence. The only way to 'realize' one's original state is to forgo the first pretence, but once one adds a second pretence to it, as far as I can see, there is no end to the series of possible pretences. I am. I pretend I am not. I pretend I am. I pretend I am not pretending to be pretending ...

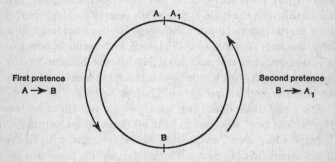

First pretence $A \rightarrow B$

Second pretence $B \rightarrow A_1$

The positions A and A_1 on the perimeter of the circle are separated by an impermeable barrier which is thinner and more transparent than one can imagine. Begin at A and move towards B. Instead of going back in a clockwise direction to A, continue in an anti-clockwise direction to point A_1. A and A_1 are 'so near and yet so far'. They are so close that one says: 'Is not A_1 just as good as A, if it is indistinguishable from A?' One may still know one is living behind an invisible veil. One cannot *see* what separates one from oneself. Anna Freud (1954) refers to a child in *When we were Very Young* by A. A. Milne.

In the nursery of this three-year-old there are four chairs. When he sits on the first, he *is* an explorer, sailing up the Amazon by night. On the second he is a lion, frightening his nurse with a roar;

on the third he is a captain, steering his ship over the sea. But on the fourth, a child's high-chair, he *tries to pretend* that he is simply himself, just a little boy (p. 89).

If or when 'he' succeeds in pretending that he is 'simply' himself, a mask will have become his face, and he himself will think that any time he acts as though he is not 'just a little boy', he is pretending *not* to be simply himself. My impression is that most three-year-olds, helped on by their parents, helped on by authorities such as Anna Freud, are well on the way to successfully pretending to be just little boys and girls. Just about this time the child abdicates his ecstasy and forgets that he is pretending to be just a little boy. He becomes just a little boy. But he is no more simply himself, because he is now just a little boy, than the man is simply himself because he *is* a waiter in a café. 'Just a little boy' is just what many authorities on children *think* a three-year-old human being *is*.

Sixty years later that man, having come to believe he was 'just a little boy' who had to learn all those things in order to become a 'big man', and having stuffed his mind with all the other things that big men tell little boys, having become a big man, begins to become an old man. But suddenly he begins to remember that it had all been a game. He had played at being a little boy, and at being a big man, and is now well into playing at being an 'old man'. His wife and children begin to get very worried. A psychoanalyst friend of the family explains that a hypomanic denial of death (he had been influenced by existentialism), is not uncommon in certain, particularly 'successful' people; it is a reversion to infantile omnipotence. Probably it can be 'contained' if he is socialized into a religious group. It might be a good idea if the minister was asked round for dinner. We'd better watch out that the investments are quite safe, just in case . . .

He *tries to pretend* that he is 'simply himself, just a little boy'. But he cannot quite do so. A three-year-old who tries and fails to pretend he is 'just a little boy' is in for trouble. He is likely to be sent for psychoanalysis if his parents can afford it. Woe betide the sixty-three-year-old man if *he* is unable to pretend that he is 'just an old man'.

In childhood, if one does not succeed in playing not to be playing when one is playing at being 'simply oneself', very soon they will get worried about infantile omnipotence going on far too long. And if sixty years later one awakens to how clever one had been to pretend so well that one has even forgotten that one has been pretending all those years, one can see clearly that they think one is getting a bit senile. Shall one try once more to pretend, this time that one is 'just a little old man?'

Jill is married to Jack. She does not want to be married to Jack. She is frightened to leave Jack. So she stays with Jack but imagines she is not married to him. Eventually she does not feel married to Jack. So she has to imagine she is. 'I have to remind myself that he is my husband.'

A common manoeuvre. Elusion is a way of getting round conflict without direct confrontation, or its resolution. It *eludes* conflict by playing off one modality of experience against another. She imagines she is *not* married and then imagines she is. Elusive spirals go on and on.

Some people[1] pretend for years that they have had gratifying sexual relations. Their lives become so based on pretence that they lose the distinction between what is really gratifying or frustrating and what they are pretending is gratifying or frustrating.

Sexual desire without sexual gratification. Jill is not entirely gratified by her private phantom relationships and yet is un-

---

1. The following account applies equally to both sexes, although for facility of statement I shall sometimes not explicitly designate both sexes. It is not only those people who are clinically categorized as hysterics or are hysterical characters who employ the manoeuvre persistently.

able sufficiently to forgo the phantom relationships to make way for the naked actual one. No 'real' relationship can be trusted not to disappoint by turning out to be false like everything else. One knows where one is with one's imagination. It does not let one down, but one gets into difficulties if one begins to *imagine* that what one imagines is real.

Phantom relationships affect bodily experience. A secret phantom lover is keeping the body irritated. This itchy excitement prompts a constant search for sexual release. Real sensations are evoked in the body by imaginary intercourse with a phantom, but it is difficult to quieten them 'in' reality. Some say they have more real feelings in imaginary situations than in real ones. Jill feels real sexual excitement in imaginary anticipation of real intercourse, but when it comes to the real thing she experiences once again no desire and no fulfilment. To live in the past or in the future may be less satisfying than to live in the present, but it can never be as disillusioning. The present will never be what has been or what could be. In the search for something outside time, there is an enervating sense of pointlessness and hopelessness.

To be sustained, elusion requires virtuosity: it can lead to enchanting nostalgia. It must never break down. If explicit, it becomes ugly. *Madame Bovary* is a definitive statement of this in literature.

Time is empty. It is as futile as it is inescapable. A false eternity, made out of all the time on one's hands which drags on eternally. It is an attempt to live outside time by living in a part of time, to live timelessly in the past, or in the future. The present is never realized.

The self of the other is eluded when the other is related to as the embodiment of phantasy. One pretends to accept the other 'as he is', but when one most thinks one is doing so, one most treats the other as embodied phantom 'as if' he or she were another person, and at the same time as if a private possession. In Winnicott's (1958) term, the other is treated as a 'transitional object'. This is yet another pretence. Self recognizes in one sense, or on one level, the other as other, as a 'person', not as a 'part-object' or as a thing, but counterfeits the full acceptance of this. It is helpful to this end if the other will collude with one's elusion and illusions. Characteristically one becomes frightened and angry to discover the other not to be the embodiment of one's phantasy prototype of the other. Living in this way, one may not lack frequent illusionment, but is likely to be subject to frequent disillusions. Each other person encountered may be seen as an oasis in the desert of one's actual life, only to turn into a mirage on getting closer. The dilution of what is, with what is not, in this elusive confusion, has the effect not of potentiating either but of diluting each, and entails some degree of depersonalization and derealization, only partly recognized. In this case one lives in a peculiar limbo. In one's flights from and towards satisfaction one may have formed 'inner' bonds with others through their imagined presence to oneself, undreamed of by more easily satisfied people. But discontent with 'mere' imagination may make one dependent on others in the hope that they will embody one's imagination and help one to elude the frightening and sinister aspects of one's phantasy. The need to seek actual others rather than imaginary others to embody one's phantasy may cause one intense involvement with people and things outside oneself. One searches in actual others for the satisfaction that eludes one in imagination, and imagines all the time the satisfactions lacking in 'reality'.

After several months of an affair begun in an atmosphere of enchantment and now pursuing a course of disenchantment and disillusion, Yvette saw the end in view. She imagined various versions of the final dramatic split-up, and discovered herself weeping bitterly in the midst of her engrossed imagining of the scene. She remarked how characteristic this was of her, that she was shedding those real tears with such intense feeling in a self-conjured-up situation that existed, as yet, only in her imagination. She predicted, quite correctly, that 'when that time came' she would feel nothing. The actual ending of her affair was prosaic and dull, without comedy or tragedy. When it finally ended she was quiet and serene for some weeks. Then retrospectively she began to dramatize the past, as she had dramatized the future. She relived in imagination a past situation which had never been more than imagined. Retrospectively the past imaginary situation became the real one. Her feelings had clicked with her present situation only in the enchanted beginning of her love affair. At other times she pretended to feel in the actual present situation and seemed only spontaneously happy or sad in imagination. Perhaps she eluded the experience of unequivocal frustration, but the price she paid was that unequivocal gratification eluded her.

Elusion, by its very nature, is difficult to pin down. That is its speciality. It counterfeits truth by a double pretence. The manoeuvre can be got into sharper focus by comparing it to some issues described in *The Divided Self* (Laing, 1960).

In that study, descriptions were given of a *modus vivendi* with some forms of anxiety and despair. In particular I described that form of self-division which involves a split of the person's being into a disembodied mind and a de-animate body. With this loss of unity, the person preserves a sense of having an 'inner' 'true' self which is, however, unrealized, whereas the 'outer', 'real', or 'actual' self is 'false'. We tried to reveal this position as a desperate attempt to come to terms with one form of 'ontological insecurity'.

The man-in-the-street takes a lot for granted: for instance, that he has a body which has an inside and an outside; that he has begun at his birth and ends biologically speaking at his death; that he occupies a position in space; that he occupies a position in time; that he exists as a continuous being from one place to the next and from one moment to the other. The ordinary person does not reflect upon these basic elements of his being; he takes his way of experiencing himself and others to be 'true'. However, some people do not. They are often called schizoid. Still more, the schizophrenic does not take for granted his own person (and other persons) as being an adequately embodied, alive, real, substantial, and continuous being, who is at one place at one time and at a different place at a different time, remaining the 'same' throughout. In the absence of this 'base' he lacks the usual sense of personal unity, a sense of himself as the agent of his own actions rather than as a robot, a machine, a *thing*, and of being the author of his own perceptions, but rather feels that someone else is using his eyes, his ears, etc.

Man is always between being and non-being, but non-being is not necessarily experienced as *personal* disintegration. The insecurity attendant upon a precariously established personal unity is *one* form of ontological insecurity, if this term is used to denote the insecurity inescapably within the heart of man's finite being.

Tillich (1952) speaks of the possibilities of non-being in the three directions of ultimate meaninglessness, ultimate condemnation, and ultimate annihilation in death. In those three directions man as a spiritual being, as a moral being, as a biological being, faces the possibility of his own annihilation, or non-being.

The ontological insecurity described in *The Divided Self* is a fourth possibility. Here, man, as a person, encounters non-being, in a preliminary form, as partial loss of the synthetic unity of self, concurrently with partial loss of relatedness with the other, and in an ultimate form, in the hypothetical end-state of *chaotic nonentity*, total loss of relatedness with self and other.

Some engage in desperate 'security operations', to use

H. S. Sullivan's phrase; others engage in sincerity operations. The whole issue is joined on a different level of experience and action, but the need of some to preserve their sincerity can undermine the security of others.

Unless one is depressed, it is the others who complain of self's lack of genuineness or sincerity. It is regarded as pathognomonic of the hysteric's characteristic strategy that his or her actions should be false, that they should be histrionic, dramatized. The hysteric, on the other hand, often insists that his feelings are real and genuine. It is we who feel that they are unreal. It is the hysteric who insists on the seriousness of his intention of committing suicide while we speak of a mere 'gesture' towards suicide. The hysteric complains that he is going to pieces. It is just in so far as we feel that he is not going to pieces, except in that he is pretending or making believe that he is, that we call him an hysteric and not a schizophrenic.

There may come a time when we claim to have realized that we have been playing a part, that we have been pretending to ourselves, that we have been trying to convince ourselves of such and such, but that now we must confess that we have not succeeded. Yet this realization or confession can very well be a further effort to 'win' by an ultimate pretence, by once more pretending the last truth about oneself, and in so doing elude its simple straightforward actual realization. One form of 'acting' is a frantic desire to make pretences real. Yet the others retain reservations. We are not convinced that all people who act in a psychotic way are 'true' schizophrenics, or 'true' manics, or 'true' melancholics, although the 'true' schizophrenic is not always easily distinguishable from the person we feel can dramatize himself into a counterfeit madness, because we tend to impute psychosis to the man who pretends to be psychotic. The act of pretence itself, if carried to extremes in that direction, tends to be regarded as mad in itself. We may feel not only that it is mad to pretend to oneself as well as to others that one is mad, but that any reason for want-ing to do so is mad. One should know the social risks if one makes a break with social reality: if one begins deliberately to make a systematic attempt not to be the self that everyone takes one to be, to escape from this identity by playing at not being there, by being anonymous, or incognito, adopting pseudonyms, saying one is dead, saying one is nobody because one's body does not belong to oneself. It is no use *pretending* that one is not just a little old man, if one has become in *phantasy* just a little old man.

The hysteric, Winnicott has suggested, is 'trying to get to a madness'. Elusion is self-generated. Madness may be sought as a way out. But although one may succeed in getting a certificate of insanity, it remains a counterfeit. The counterfeit can engulf one's life as much as the 'real thing'. But 'real' madness can be as elusive as 'real' sanity. Not all who would can be psychotic.

CHAPTER 4

The Counterpoint of Experience

REAL bodily excitement, together with imaginary experiences, holds for many a specific fascination mixed with horror.

A boy is excited by seeing 'attractive' girls. He conjures them up in imagination. Real intercourse may for a time be not so much desired as imaginary intercourse with 'real' orgasm.

Sartre (1952) regards an 'honest' masturbator as one who masturbates for want of anything more actual. He describes what he regards as 'dishonest' masturbation in his discussion of Jean Genet.

A masturbator by choice, Genet prefers his own caresses since the enjoyment received coincides with the enjoyment given, the moment of passivity with that of the greatest activity; he is at one and the same time this consciousness that clots (*caille*) and this hand which churns in agitation. Being, existence; faith, works; masochistic inertia and sadistic ferocity; petrification and liberty; at the moment of pleasure the two contradictory components of Genet coincide; he is the criminal who violates and the saint who lets himself be violated. The masturbator makes himself unreal – he brings about his own rerealisation; he is very near to discovering the magic formula that will open the sluice gates.

However, victim of execution, caresser or caressed, these phantasies in the end will have to be reabsorbed into Narcissus; Narcissus fears men, their judgements, and their real presence; he wishes only to experience an aura of love for himself, he asks only to be slightly distanced from his own body, only for there to be a light coating of otherness over his flesh and over his thoughts. His personae are melting sweets; this lack of consistency reassures him and serves his sacrilegious designs: it caricatures love. The masturbator is enchanted at never being able to feel himself sufficiently another, and at producing for himself alone the diabolic appearance of a couple that fades away when one touches it. The failure of pleasure is the acid of pleasure of failure. Masturbation as a pure demonic act sustains in the heart of consciousness an appearance of appearance: masturbation is the derealisation of the world and of the masturbator himself. But this man who is eaten up by his own dream knows surely enough that this dream is there only by virtue of his willing it; Divine (the other in some of Genet's masturbation phantasies) ceaselessly absorbs Genet into herself, and Genet ceaselessly absorbs Divine. However, by a reversal which brings ecstasy to a point of overflowing, this clear negation (*clair néant*) will provoke real events in the true world; the cause of the erection, the ejaculation, the damp stains on the bedclothes is – the *imaginary*. In a single movement the masturbator captures the world to dissolve it and insert the order of the unreal into the universe; it is necessary that they *be* the images, since they *act*. No, the masturbation of Narcissus is not, as some misguidedly think, the little gallantry that one performs toward the evening, the nice, boyish compensation for a day's work: *it wills itself a crime*. Genet draws his pleasure from his nothingness: solitude, impotence, the unreal, evil, have produced, without recourse to being, an event in the world (pp. 341–2).

Not all who would, Sartre remarks elsewhere, can be Narcissus. For Narcissus, who relies on the image as the exquisitely fragile link between his divided selves, masturbation is the act of choice. For Genet, the other is conjured up only to be conjured away, together with himself, in his act of masturbation – and when the spell is ended there remains only Genet, and yet it is only in virtue of these phantom homosexual essences, distilled into images, that Genet himself exists. 'I exist only through those who are nothing apart from the being they have through me.'

Here, we find a further elusion. In the evocation of the unreal presence of the other in imagination, what we still call phantasy is resonated. Phantasy and the imaginary are merged so that it is no longer possible to know when masturbation begins or ends. The real blends with imagination, imagination with phantasy, and phantasy with the real.

The masturbator has a body that experiences real orgasms in imaginary situations, but *real* orgasm may be necessary to end the imaginary situation.

Imagination induces real physical effects, but these are subtly different from the experience of a non-imaginary relationship. Thus, accustomed to the orgasm of masturbation, he becomes unsure of how to handle his body in non-imaginary relations. The masturbator may then feel awkward, gauche, self-conscious, fearful that he will get inappropriately 'turned on' in the real presence of others. He is afraid that his body will start to react as it does 'in' imagination. There may be a big difference between how his body feels to him and how it appears to others. But the mingling of non-imaginary feelings with imaginary others in orgasm may lead him to fear their confusion in a public situation.

If the body is privately aroused in relation to imaginary others, may it not be aroused by non-imaginary others? If this private body, a guilty experience in the intimacy of solitude, begins to be evoked publicly, one's experience is profoundly modified. The man sees the woman coloured by his experience of her as imagined in intercourse with his solitary body. This masturbatory mingling of his body and her imagined body is resonated in a real relation to her, and he goes on to expect her to see *his* body in the light of how he feels it, and to expect her to realize the way he imagines *her* in his masturbatory imagination.

Thus one young man bumped into a girl in the corridor whom he had just been fucking in the office lavatory, and was so embarrassed that he had to give up that job.

Consider this description by Ferenczi (1938) of woman's sexuality. The activity and experience described are a blend of phantasy and imagination, incarnated in flesh. It is possible that this woman is *unable* to masturbate alone, because she needs another to embody her phantasies. We take Ferenczi's account as a description of a *possible* woman, not, as he meant it, as a description of contemporary femininity.

The development of genital sexuality (in the woman) is characterised above all else by the displacement of erogenity from the clitoris (the female penis) to the cavity of the vagina. Psychoanalytic experience compels the assumption, however, that not alone the vagina but, in the manner of hysteria, other parts of the body as well are genitalised, in particular the nipple and the surrounding area ... the partly abandoned male striving to return to the maternal womb is not altogether given up, at any rate in the psychic sphere, where it expresses itself as a phantasied identification in coitus with the penis-possessing male, and as the vaginal sensation of possessing a penis ('hollow penis'), as well as an identification on the part of the woman with the child that she harbours within her own body. Masculine aggressiveness turns into a passive pleasure in experiencing the sex act (masochism), which is explicable in part on the ground of very archaic instinctual forces (the death instinct of Freud), in part on that of the mechanism of identification with the conquering male. All these secondary recathexes of spatially remote and genetically superseded pleasure mechanisms in the female sex seem to have been instituted more or less by way of consolation for the loss of the penis.

Of the transition on the part of the woman from (masculine) activity to passivity one may form the following general idea; the genitality of the female penis is absorbed regressively into the whole body and into the whole ego of the woman, out of which – amphimictically, as we believe – it had arisen, so that a secondary narcissism becomes her portion; on the erotic side, therefore, she becomes again more like a child who wants to be loved, and is thus a being who still clings *in toto* to the fiction of existence in the mother's womb. In this way she can then easily identify herself with the child in her own body (or with the penis as its symbol) and make the transition from the transitive to the intransitive, from active penetration to passivity. The secondary genitalisation of the female body also explains her greater proneness to conversion hysteria.

To observe the genital development of the female is to obtain the impression that on the occasion of the first sexual intercourse this development is still quite uncompleted. The first attempts at coitus are so to speak only acts of rape in which even blood must flow. It is only later that the woman learns to experience the sex act passively, and later still to feel it as pleasurable or even to take an active part in it. Indeed, in the individual sex act the initial defence is repeated in the form of a muscular resistance on the part of the narrowed vagina; it is only later that the vagina becomes lubricated and easy of entrance, and only later still that there occur the contractions which seem to have as their purpose the aspiration of the semen and the incorporation of the penis – the latter certainly an intended castration as well. These observations, together with certain phylogenetic considerations which will occupy us more fully later, suggested to me the conception that one phase of the warfare between the sexes is here repeated individually – a phase in which the woman comes off second best, since she cedes to the man the privilege of penetrating the mother's body in a real sense, while she herself contents herself with phantasy-like substitutes, and particularly with harbouring the child whose fortune she shares. At all events, according to the psychoanalytic observations of Groddeck, there is vouchsafed to the female, even in childbirth and hidden behind the painfulness of labour, a meed of pleasure which is denied to the male sex (pp. 24–6).

In this description, the woman's own bodily experiences are so buried under phantasy that she is almost completely alienated from her own real feminine bodily experience. Ferenczi sees her as 'lost' in phantasy, and in the imaginary. One should not confuse these two categories. It would not be accurate to say that she 'imagines' that she has a penis. She might be shocked at the thought, and never dared imagine such a thing. 'In phantasy' she is a man; 'in imagination' she is a woman. She has not discovered her own body. By imagining herself to be a woman, and acting as though she were a woman, she is trying to become a woman. She is using her imagination and her flesh to try to extricate herself from phantasy, but seems only to take her phantasy to be more and more real, the less she recognizes her phantasies.

Ferenczi's woman is a stranger to her own non-phantasy and non-imaginary feminine body experience because she is lost in her phantasy. If her phantasy of having a penis becomes sufficiently 'real', she will imagine not that she has a penis, but that she has *not* got one. Imagination is then used to imagine what one has not got in phantasy. It is another form of counterfeit. She does not *know* that what she experiences is phantasy. Her phantasy body, unrecognized as such, casts a veil over her 'own' body, so that the act of intercourse is, in a sense, an act of masturbation for her.

Although masturbation may be dishonest in so far as it is a negation of the real, the 'real' can be used dishonestly to mask the secret play of phantasy and imagination. Masturbation counterfeits intercourse as intercourse counterfeits masturbation.

The following passage is from *Our Lady of the Flowers* (Genet, 1957a).

Something different, a kind of feeling of power, sprang up (in the vegetal, germinative sense) in Divine. She thought she had been virilized. A wild hope made her strong and husky and vigorous. She felt muscles growing, and felt herself emerging from a rock carved by Michael Angelo in the form of a slave. Without moving a muscle, though straining within herself, she struggled internally just as Laocoön seizes the monster and twists it. Then, bolder still, she wanted to box, with her arms and legs of flesh, but she very quickly got knocked about on the boulevard, for she judged and willed her movements not in accordance with their combative efficiency but rather in accordance with an aesthetic that would have made of her a hoodlum of a more or less gallant stripe. Her movements, particularly a hitching of the belt and her guard position, were meant, whatever the cost, at the cost of victory itself, to make of her not the boxer Divine, but a certain admired boxer, and at times several fine boxers rolled into one. She tried for male gestures, which are rarely the gestures of males. She whistled, put her hands into her pockets, and this whole performance was carried out so unskilfully that in the course of a single evening she seemed to be four or five characters at the same time. She thereby acquired the richness of a multiple personality. She ran from boy to girl, and the transitions from one to the other – because the attitude was a new one – were made stumblingly. She would hop after the boy on one foot. She would always begin her Big Scatterbrain gestures, then, suddenly remembering that she was supposed to show she was virile so as to captivate the murderer, she would end by burlesquing them, and this double formula enveloped her in strangeness, made her a timid clown in plain dress, a sort of embittered swish. Finally, to crown her metamorphosis from female into tough male, she imagined a man to man friendship which would link her with one of those faultless pimps whose gestures could not be regarded as ambiguous. And to be on the safe side, she invented Marchetti. It was a simple matter to choose a physique for him, for she possessed in her secret, lonely-girl's imagination, for her nights' pleasure, a stock of thighs, arms, torsoes, faces, hair, teeth, necks and knees, and she knew how to assemble them so as to make of them a live man to whom she loaned a soul – which was always the same one for each of these constructions: the one she would have liked to have herself (pp. 89–90).

Genet describes a *man* whom he calls 'Divine' as 'she', since 'in phantasy' this is how he experiences himself. At one point, 'she' begins 'in a vegetal, germinative sense' to feel a new virility within 'her'. 'She' does not 'imagine' this: it happens to 'her' – but it does not go far: as this sexual transformation peters out, 'she' pretends (literally: stretches out ahead of herself to grasp something in anticipation) that 'she' is a man. 'She' uses 'her' imagination, gestures, actions, to regain by a magical metamorphosis 'her' lost masculinity. But 'she' is trying to make ice by boiling water.

Dostoyevsky's genius is unmistakable in his grasp of the counterpoint of dreams, phantasy, imagination, and memory. All his novels reveal or imply simultaneous participation in these modalities. It is not easy to demonstrate this succinctly. We shall try to do so, by considering Dostoyevsky's account of Raskolnikov at the beginning of *Crime and Punishment* in terms of dream, phantasy, imagination, reality, up to and including the murder.

The modality of 'phantasy' in contrast to 'imagination' is shown clearly in Raskolnikov.

The day before he murders the old woman, Raskolnikov 'dreamed a terrible dream' (1951, p. 72, et seq.). This is a long, intricate, vivid dream. We abridge it drastically.

... He dreamed of the time when he was a child and when they still lived in their little provincial town. He was a boy of seven. It was a holiday, late in the afternoon, and he was out for a walk in the country with his father.

His father and he were walking along a road to a cemetery, where were the graves of his grandmother and a brother who had died at the age of six months, whom Raskolnikov could not remember. They were passing a pub; he was holding his father's hand and gazing fearfully at the pub, which was associated with scenes of drunkenness and violence. In front of the pub there was a large cart such as would usually be pulled by a large drayhorse...

... but now, curiously enough, some peasant's small, lean, greyish-brown mare was harnessed to one of these huge carts, the sort of poor old nag which – he had seen it so often – found it very hard to draw quite an ordinary cart with wood or hay piled on top of it, especially when the cart was stuck in the mud or in a rut, and every time that happened, the peasant flogged her so brutally, so brutally, sometimes even across the eyes and muzzle, and he felt so sorry, so sorry for the poor old horse that he almost burst into tears, and his mother always used to take him away from the window. But now in front of the pub pandemonium suddenly broke loose: a crowd of blind drunk big peasants in red and blue shirts with their coats thrown over their shoulders came out of the pub, yelling and singing and strumming their balalaikas. 'Come on, get on my cart!' shouted one of them, quite a young peasant with a terribly thick neck and a very red, beefy face. 'I'll drive you all home! Get in!'

The poor old nag is unequal to the task imposed on her. The peasants find this a great joke:

... People were laughing, and indeed, how could they help laughing? The mare was all skin and bones, and there she was supposed to drag such a heavy load at a gallop! Two young lads in the cart at once took a whip each and got ready to help Mikolka.

They begin to flog her.

'Daddy! Daddy!' he cried to his father. 'Daddy, look what they are doing! Daddy, they're beating the poor little horse!'

'Come along, come along, son,' said his father. 'They're drunk. Having fun, the fools. Come along and don't look,' and he tried to take him away, but he tore himself out of his father's hands and hardly realizing what he was doing, ran to the old horse. But the poor old mare was already in a very bad state. She was gasping for breath, standing still, pulling at the cart again, and almost collapsing in the road.

'Flog her to death!' shouted Mikolka. 'I don't mind. I'm going to flog her to death myself!'

The joke becomes more hilarious as Mikolka's fury mounts. He shouts that she is his property.

'I'll damn well do what I like with her! Come on, there's plenty of room. Come on, all of you! I'm going to make her gallop if it's the last thing I do!'

Only the seven-year-old Raskolnikov feels concern for the poor old nag.

He ran beside the old mare, he ran in front of her, he saw her being whipped across her eyes, across the very eyes! He was crying. His heart heaved. Tears rolled down his cheeks. One of the men who were flogging the horse grazed his face with the whip, but he felt nothing. Wringing his hands and screaming, he rushed up to the old man with the grey beard who was shaking his head and condemning it all. A woman took him by the hand and tried to lead him away, but he freed himself and ran back to the poor old horse, which seemed to be at the last gasp, but started kicking once more.

'Oh, to hell with you!' shouted Mikolka furiously, and, throwing down his whip, he bent down and dragged out a long thick shaft from the bottom of the cart. Taking hold of it by one end with both hands, he swung it with an effort over the grey-brown mare.

'He'll strike her dead!' they shouted all round. 'He'll kill her!'

'My property!' shouted Mikolka, and let fall the shaft with all his might. There was the sound of a heavy thud.

'Flog her! Flog her! Why have you stopped?' Shouts were heard in the crowd.

And Mikolka swung the shaft another time, and another terrific blow fell across the back of the unhappy mare. She subsided on her haunches, but presently was on her feet again, pulling, pulling with all her remaining strength first on one side and then on another, trying to move the cart. But they were belabouring her from every side with six whips, and the shaft was raised again and fell for the third and then for the fourth time, slowly and with terrific force. Mikolka was furious because he had not been able to kill her with one blow.

'Alive and kicking!' they shouted on all sides.

'Bet she'll fall down any minute now, lads,' shouted a sportsman in the crowd. 'She's about finished!'

'Why don't you strike her with an axe? Despatch her at once!' a third one shouted.

'Oh, damn her! Make way!' Mikolka yelled furiously and, throwing down the shaft, he once more bent down in the cart and pulled out an iron bar. 'Mind!' he shouted, swinging it with all his might over the poor old horse. The bar came down with a crash;

the old mare swayed, subsided, and was about to give another pull at the cart when the bar once again descended on her back with terrific force, and she collapsed on the ground as though her four legs had given way from under her all at once.

'Finish her off!' Mikolka shouted, jumping down from the cart, blind with rage.

A few young men, also red-faced and drunk, seized whatever they could lay their hands on – whips, sticks, the shaft – and ran to the dying mare. Mikolka stood on one side and started raining blows across her back with the iron bar without bothering to see where the blows were falling. The mare stretched out her head, heaved a deep sigh, and died.

'Settled her!' they shouted in the crowd.

'Why didn't she gallop?'

'My property!' shouted Mikolka, iron bar in hand and with bloodshot eyes. He stood there as though he were sorry he had nothing more to flog.

'Aye, you ain't got the fear of God in you after all,' many voices were already shouting in the crowd.

But by now the poor little boy was beside himself. He pushed his way through the crowd to the grey-brown mare, put his arms round her dead, bloodstained muzzle, and kissed her, kissed her on the eyes, on the lips. ... Then suddenly jumped to his feet and rushed in a rage at Mikolka with his little fists. But just then his father, who had been running after him, caught hold of him at last and carried him out of the crowd.

'Come along, son, come along,' he said to him. 'Let's go home.'

'Daddy, why – why did they kill the poor little horse?' he whimpered, but suddenly his breath failed him and the words came in shrieks from his panting breast.

'They're drunk,' said his father. 'Playing the fool. It's not our business. Come along!'

He put his arms round his father, but his chest tightened and he felt choked. He tried to draw a breath, to cry out and – woke up.

Raskolnikov woke up in a cold sweat, his hair wet with perspiration, gasping for breath, and he raised himself in terror.

'Thank God it was only a dream!' he said, sitting down under a tree and drawing deep breaths. 'But what's the matter with me? These are not the symptoms of a fever, are they? What a horrible dream!'

Every bone in his body seemed to ache; his soul was in confusion and darkness. He put his elbows on his knees and propped his head on his hands.

'Good God!' he cried, 'Is it possible that I will really take a hatchet, hit her on the head with it, crack her skull, slither about in warm, sticky blood, break the lock, steal and shake with fear, hide myself all covered in blood and with the hatchet – Good God! Is it possible?'

Raskolnikov's first experience on waking shows that his own body is intimately compromised by this dream. He awoke in terror as though it was *he* who had been flogged to death, and immediately recalls with horror his intention to kill the old woman by hitting her on the head in a very similar way to the striking of the old nag.

From this, it seems that Raskolnikov's experience of his 'own' body is in terms of a physical identification with the old mare and the old woman. The site of the incident is close to the cemetery wherein are the graves of his grandmother and younger brother. He does not '*imagine*' himself to be an old mare/old woman. On the contrary, 'in his imagination' he is as far as possible from the situation in which he is in his dream or in his phantasy. In his dream he is a seven-year-old boy empathizing with an old nag, while in phantasy his own body participates in the death of an old nag and old woman. But 'he', we learn later, imagines himself to be Napoleon! He is 'lost' between his imagination, where he thinks of himself as Napoleon, his dream, where he is a little boy, and his phantasy, where he is a beaten old mare and an old woman he is about to kill.

Raskolnikov is aware of his dreams and of his intention to murder the old woman money-lender. He is not aware of the link between Mikolka and the other ruthlessly violent drunken peasants and himself, or of the link between the old mare and the old woman. He does not connect the above with his 'own' feelings towards his mother.[1] He is not aware of identifying his mother (or grandmother) with a miserly money-lender and with an old nag that is good for nothing. Nor is he aware of identifying him*self* with the old nag, his mother, or the money-lender.

When he finally 'knows' that the old woman will be murdered tomorrow, he feels himself like a man sentenced to death. In the modality of his phantasy, *he* is the victim, whereas 'in imagination' and in 'reality' he is the executioner.

Just before he enters the gates of the old woman's flat to kill her, he remarks about his own thoughts: 'It's like that, I suppose, that the thoughts of those who are led to execution cling to everything they see on the way. . . .' That is, in phantasy he is more the victim being led to execution than the executioner.

Just before the old woman opens her door he suddenly loses the feel of his own body. It appears that in order to murder this old woman, his action-in-phantasy is to re-project 'the old nag' on to the person of the money-lender who 'in reality' means nothing to him.

Raskolnikov murders the old woman 'to be Napoleon', 'for money', or just 'for spite' as he later speculates. But Dostoyevsky discloses also his phantasy, a modality of action and experience, as a *physical dream,* in which he is submerged and contained. Thus in bondage he is estranged, with transitory moments of emergence, from participation in the 'real' world as a young man in his 'own' person. In this state, recognition of who the other is remains unavailable to him.

In this novel, the theme of the prostitute is deeply explored. The old woman is yet another *pro*-stitute, as is Raskolnikov himself, in the sense of one who stands for another. Dostoyevsky

1. See Chapter 10.

makes clear that Raskolnikov conceived a violent aversion to her 'at once, though he knew nothing about her'. The 'old woman' and her sister were experienced so much in the modality of phantasy that little else registered on Raskolnikov. Awareness that he was *phantasizing* them rather than *perceiving* them 'in their own light' was fugitive. He was trapped 'within' his phantasy. No wonder he felt stifled.

CHAPTER 5

The Coldness of Death

THE following account of the experiences of a thirty-four-year-old woman, shortly after the birth of her third child, covers a period of five months. During these months the blend of phantasy, dream, and imagination constituted a puerperal psychosis which was, clinically speaking, not unusual.

Although her doctor had been unable to find any organic illness, Mrs A was still unable to get up from bed three weeks after her third baby had been born. After her two previous pregnancies she had felt something of the same exhaustion, a complete disinclination to do anything, and no interest in the familiar people and things of her life.

One night 'a terrible storm' raged in her head. Sails seemed to crackle and tear in the wind. Although this may have been what we call a dream, she was convinced that she had not slept for a moment. When her husband came home the following day from a business trip, she accused him of having ruined her by her repeated pregnancies and said he was callous and cruel. She had never expressed any feelings of this kind before. She was completely exhausted and was unable to carry on with the care of the baby or in any way look after the other two children. The doctor was called and, although he could find no physical signs, diagnosed cystitis and prescribed pills. She did not take these pills until the following night, because she was afraid that they might not cure her, or even that in her state they might do her harm. This attitude made those about her think for the first time that she was 'mental'.

However, in the evening she got up and behaved normally when friends came round but she had a distinct, though indescribable, feeling of being 'different', which she attributed to her toxic condition. She spent another awful night with a violent storm inside her, with again sails flapping in her head and, in addition, a peculiar sense of her thoughts running down and coming to a standstill. When she awoke from a fitful sleep she no longer felt that she had a fever, as she had done. A 'realization' swept over her that nothing had anything to do with her – she was no longer in 'that' world. The room and the baby in the cot suddenly appeared small and far away 'as though seen through the wrong end of a telescope'. She felt completely unconcerned. She was 'absolutely and completely emotionless'.

As she lay in this state, peculiar sensations developed in her tongue. It seemed paralysed and twisted. She looked at her tongue in a mirror: it looked normal, but the discrepancy between how it felt and how it looked frightened her. By mid-morning she was beginning to think she was poisoned and that the poison was coursing through her blood-stream. She took her temperature. The fact that it was normal was because her body was not reacting to the poison.

The idea of a poison in her blood persisted throughout the next five months and found expression in various dreams that she had in the transitional period when she was half in and half out of her state of 'non-reaction'. She believed at first that the poison came from a germ in her bladder; some weeks later she developed a cold and then came to believe that the second germ, the cold germ, had killed and replaced the first one. Later still she thought that the poison came from her bowels, perhaps from intestinal worms. There was no one word that served to convey entirely to her satisfaction what she felt she had inside her. A germ, a worm, a 'little beast' was poisoning her and causing her body to decay.

She was in 'the coldness of death'. The extremities of her limbs were cold: there was a weight in her arms and legs. It was an enormous effort to make the slightest movement. Her chest was empty. In this state near death she was as much concerned for the doctors as for herself, for they would get into terrible trouble after her death for misdiagnosing her case. The doctors were tragically deluded by the absence of physical signs of her death. The absence of such signs was the mark of her absolutely unique condition. Because her body was in a state of 'non-reaction', it was entirely logical that the doctors should find absolutely no abnormality. She could hardly blame them for their tragically mistaken conclusions; she wished that both she and the doctors should be correct, but she was afraid that that was impossible. When she had died the poison lying in her body would give the impression that she had committed suicide, but when the full facts came to light she might be just that unique case which could well revolutionize the whole of medical science. Then the doctors who had been in attendance on her would suffer extreme disgrace. Although she complained of complete exhaustion, she was prepared to talk about her dying state indefinitely, and her movements were not slowed up.

To her, her skin had a dying pallor. Her hands were unnaturally blue, almost black. Her heart might stop at any moment. Her bones felt twisted and in a powder. Her flesh was decaying. After she came back from that world of death to this world of life, she described the beginning of the end as follows:

One day, about the middle of March, I became conscious of the dreadful coldness in my legs but at the same time noticed that my feet were warm. This didn't make sense to me in the light of my own hypothesis and it made me think. I got no inspiration, however, but some days later, while sitting thinking of nothing in particular, I thought of the fact that any illness sufficiently serious to make one 'start' to die would first of all prostrate the person regardless of the strength of that person's will-power. I felt very bucked at this idea, but nevertheless needed the assurance of a doctor that it was a correct conclusion, and it didn't really afford me much relief as there was still, in my mind, far too much to counterbalance it and I was still incapable of holding on to thoughts for any length of time. Shortly after that I saw the ridiculousness of my idea of a condition of 'starting to die', and realized that I was talking of a dying state synonymous with stopping reacting to a fever which would result in death in a matter of hours (so I presumed). I still felt very ill, as if I had pneumonia and was made to walk about with it, especially when made to go outside, and felt my heartbeat very, very weak and my respiration very shallow and my hands going blue at times other than when put in water. I got slight agitation and a feeling of losing my grip and one night in bed got a sudden thought that I was indeed in a state of unreality and that I was about to come out of it, and panicked at the thought of coming out of it – felt overwhelmed and weak. I curled up, decided to hold on to it, and the feeling passed.

Shortly after that I found the psychological explanation for the blueness in my hands, and a week later for the action of splashing water on my hands to induce the blueness and the necessity to apply soap to make a lather. I felt very well that night, could breathe deeply, felt warm all over, and felt my pulse strong. The following morning, I felt happy at the prospect of another day and didn't consider the possibility of dying during it, but had twinges of pain all over my body, particularly in my wrists and my head. The following day again I was back where I started, felt all my symptoms most acutely, and was thoroughly convinced that my own diagnosis was the correct one. This state of mind continued for a week during which my efforts to the doctors to prove myself correct were as strong as ever. At the end of that week I went out for the first weekend, not because I felt any better, but because I couldn't keep putting my girl-friend off any longer, and I was thoroughly fed up with my position in the hospital and felt I couldn't be worse. While out, I found that I felt normal in the presence of people, no longer felt a barrier between me and them, and again couldn't reconcile the fact with my idea of being in a dying state. Nevertheless, I still felt death to be imminent all the time and spent the rest of the week striving to prove my point. I decided myself to go out for the next weekend, as I was absolutely fed up with my surroundings and with the psychiatrist and felt agitated and frightened with the goings-on in the ward and wanted to escape from it all. During that weekend I was able to reassure myself each time I panicked within myself, all the arguments against my own hypothesis occurred to me at the same time and I felt that the explanation for the blueness in my hands was really a true and correct one. Therefore when, on my return to the hospital, the psychiatrist suggested that I become an outpatient I was very pleased, though I still felt all my symptoms except the coldness in my legs, and I was surprised to find that I could have an emotion of pleasure. I got an intense urge to escape from the drabness of my surroundings in the hospital: I was feeling very ill at ease [*sic*] in the ward in the knowledge of the uncertainty of the patients' behaviour. Even if I did feel very ill, I thought it pleasanter to be so in the more pleasant environment of a dwelling house with normal people. I found myself responding to music and appreciating cartoons and anything humorous and enjoying reading and not necessarily medical articles – I had become definitely positive in thought. Nevertheless, I got frequent panics and while in them couldn't see beyond my feelings of the moment, which were those of collapsing and dying, but when it came time for me to make the journey to the hospital alone I was able to put my trust in God and derived absolute confidence from the psychiatrist's faith in my ability to do this, and was determined not to let him or myself down. I became more and more optimistic and then one morning, had a flash of realization of the doctor's ability to diagnose a dying state regardless of what caused it, and with that I saw clearly that I had been deluded and knew that I was so no longer. After that, each day brought an improvement, and I became less and less apathetic and began to desire to go home to see my husband and children. I was completely disinterested in my symptoms and was able to see very clearly what had happened to me and how it had all come about.

The 'psychological' explanation of the blue-blackness of her hands occurred as a 'flash' of 'realization'. Her hands were her second baby, over whose blue-black face she had once splashed cold water when it was in the midst of a breath-holding attack.

She now had numerous 'flashes' when she emerged briefly from what she called the 'tapestry of symbols' in which her whole body was enveloped. Thus she had a sudden 'realization' as she lay awake at night anxiously listening for her next heartbeat, that her heart *was* a foetus, whose heart was beating faintly and rapidly, and in the next four weeks she 'realized' that her twisted tongue *was* her father's tongue after he had had a stroke: that her skin and chest were those of her brother as she watched him die of tuberculosis. She emerged in these 'realizations' from her 'state of unreality', but sometimes lapsed into her unreal state despite herself. Sometimes, as she writes above, she desperately clutched at her 'unreality', and the whiff of reality passed by. She had a number of dreams that seemed to be on these issues, among others.

In one dream she was cornered by a man who was going to assault her. There seemed no escape. She was at her wits' end when, still in the dream, she tried to escape into a waking consciousness, but she continued to be cornered, in fact it was now worse because it was real, so she escaped back into dreaming that 'it was only a dream anyway'. In another dream she was inside a dark house looking out of a doorway across which was laid a black umbrella. In the dream she felt that inside was unreality and outside was reality, but she was barred from getting outside because of the umbrella. A third dream, just after she had finally emerged from 'the coldness of death', had the following elements: She was outside looking at a large aeroplane; in the doorway of the aeroplane stood a doctor who embodied elements of various people including myself. This time she had a conviction that outside was reality and inside was unreality. She wanted to get inside into unreality but the doctor barred her way. She summarized the five months of her death state: 'I seem to have been living in a metaphorical state. I wove a tapestry of symbols and have been living in it.'

After coming out of this metaphorical state, in which she had lived in a state of near death, in her own tapestry of symbols, she felt much more keenly alive than she could remember. Five years later, she still felt well and had had another child without complications.

Why people go into states of this kind we do not know. The keynote of hers was 'the coldness of death'. She never actually went through the door to feel that she *was* dead. She was different, remote, gone into another world. This world came to be *that* world. Her skin, her tongue, her hands, her lungs, heart, bladder, intestines, her blood, her bones, were drawn into the domain of death. She came back from that world of the dead and unreality, to this world of the living, in flashes of realization. She came back in the spring, after the strangest winter of her life.

But as she came back she was released from more than the deathly captivity of the past five months. She felt in her successive realizations that her body had been occupied by the bodies of the dead: (the one exception was her heart, which she had actually felt stop beating when for a moment she had thought her baby was dead); and that this had been the state of affairs for some time before she began to feel the coldness of death; and that through rediscovering her own body, which had become a sort of graveyard wherein were buried bits of her father, brother, and mother, she had in a sense arisen from the dead. She had come back to life, from the realm of the dead.

I have alluded elsewhere to the possibility that what we call psychosis may be sometimes a natural process of healing (a view for which I claim no priority).

Confronted with this woman's experience, clinical psychiatric terminology, in both its descriptive and theoretical aspects, is almost completely inadequate. Unless one can describe, one cannot explain.

One glimpses here the naked, intricate actuality of the complexity of experiences that those of us who do not deny what we cannot explain or even describe are struggling to understand. Theory can only legitimately be made on behalf of experience, not in order to deny experience which the theory ignores out of embarrassment. The following description is only the first step in a phenomenological analysis.

Mrs A's habitual way of experiencing her husband, children, and friends faded rapidly and was replaced by a new way of experiencing. She went out of this world into another world where she was enveloped in a tapestry of symbols. What we regard as 'real' ceased to mean anything to her. However, at the time her experiences did not *feel unreal*. She did not complain at the time she was in the coldness of death that she experienced her body, or other people, in an unreal way. It was only when she was coming out of what she had been in, that, looking back, she 'realized' she had been living in a state of 'unreality', *as she put it*.

Our habitual sense of being related to others, of being ourselves 'connected', of being real and alive, is often supported by a phantasy modality of which we are unaware. Phantasy is not usually experienced as unreal. 'Real' and alive, in contrast to 'unreal' and dead, are more qualities of phantasy than of imagination. Being in love may be an experience largely 'in' phantasy, and nothing may be more real or alive.

When she began to go into 'the coldness of death', Mrs A no longer felt a personal bond between her present self and her old world. She came uncoupled from that old world in which she could see her husband, children, and friends still were. This detachment was not the consequence, as far as I could assess, of any intention on her part. Even were she to have consciously intended to withdraw from the world, how did it happen to her when most people who wish intensely to get away from themselves and from the world *cannot* do so?

The following two columns list some of the links she made in her 'flashes' of realization. She made them herself. They were as complete a surprise to me as they were to her. No interpretations remotely resembling them had come from anyone.

Her tongue felt as twisted, but seen as normal	was	her father's tongue when he had a series of strokes that ended his life.
Her chest felt as empty, and her skin seen as yellow	were	her brother's chest and skin on his deathbed.
Her hand seen as blue-black	was	her baby's head in a breath-holding attack.
Her heart	was	her baby during her last pregnancy when there had been anxiety about something going wrong.
Her bones	were	the bones of her mother, who had been crippled with rheumatoid arthritis since the patient's early childhood.

In the coldness of death nothing was more real than that she was in a dying state, and would die like her father, mother, or brother. Nothing was less real than the relation between her tongue, chest, hands, heart, bones, with her father, mother, brother, or baby.[1]

1. Consider the sequence: night, storm, worm, sickness unto death. Compare this with the sequence in Blake's poem.

O Rose, thou art sick!
The invisible worm
That flies in the night,
In the howling storm.

Critical experiences with the latter set, the domain, had been mapped on to parts of her body, the range. Through the mapping operation of introjective identification, these parts of her body had acquired a ϕ-value. She reacted to them in terms of their ϕ-value, unaware that her experience of them was a product of mapping. *How* she could perform this operation, and sustain it, and by what further operation she could eliminate the former operation from her experience, I do not know.

———————

> Has found out thy bed
> Of crimson joy,
> And his dark secret love
> Does thy life destroy.

The parallel is nearly complete.

Part Two

Forms of Interpersonal Action

CHAPTER 6

Complementary Identity

Rabbi Kabia (in Roman captivity) to his favourite pupil, Simeon ben Yochai: 'My son, more than a calf wishes to suck, does the cow yearn to suckle.'

In accounts of experience and action in imagination, dream, and phantasy, it is always necessary to extend our account explicitly or by implication to a whole 'nexus' of others, imaginary, dreamed, phantasied, or 'real'. I shall try to bring the relation between these others and self into sharper relief.

The most significant theoretical and methodological development in the psychiatry of the last two decades is, in my view, the growing dissatisfaction with any theory or study of the individual which isolates him from his context. Efforts have been made from different angles to remedy this position. One may note, however, that there are formidable pitfalls. A schema may falsely fragment reality. There is a distinction between fragmentation that does violence to personal reality, and a legitimate analysis of one aspect of a situation at a time. One does not wish to sever 'mind' and 'body', 'psychic' and 'physical'. One must not treat 'persons' as 'animals' or 'things', but one would be foolish to try to disrupt man from his relation to other creatures and from the matter that is his matrix. It is immensely difficult not to subject unwittingly our human reality to such conceptual mutilation that the original is lost in the process.

Moreover, we cannot give an undistorted account of 'a person' without giving an account of his relation with others. Even an account of one person cannot afford to forget that each person is always *acting* upon others and *acted upon* by others. The others are there also. No one acts or experiences in a vacuum. The person whom we describe, and over whom we theorize, *is not the only agent in his 'world'*. How he perceives and acts towards the others, how they perceive and act towards him, how he perceives them as perceiving him, how they perceive him as perceiving them, are all aspects of 'the situation'. They are all pertinent to understanding one person's participation in it.

COMPLEMENTARITY

A woman cannot be a mother without a child. She needs a child to give her the identity of a mother. A man needs a wife for him to be a husband. A lover without a beloved is only a would-be lover. Tragedy or comedy, according to the point of view. All 'identities' require an other: some other in and through a relationship with whom self-identity is actualized. The other by his or her actions may impose on self an unwanted identity. The husband who is a cuckold may have had this identity imposed on him despite himself.

By complementarity[1] I denote that function of personal relations whereby the other fulfils or completes self. One person may complement another in many different senses. This function is biologically determined at one level, and a matter of

1. This use of the term complementarity is to be distinguished from other current usages. For instance Haley (1958b) contrasts 'complementary' with 'symmetrical' relationships.

'A complementary relationship consists of one person giving and the other receiving rather than the two competing as in a symmetrical relationship. In a complementary relationship the two people are of unequal status, one is in a superior position and the other is in a secondary position. A "superior" position means that the person initiates action and the other follows that action; he offers criticism and the other accepts it, he offers advice and the other assumes that he should, and so on. In such a relationship the two people tend to fit together or complement each other' (p. 44).

This concept is not the same.

highly individualized choice at the other extreme. Complementarity is more or less formalized, culturally conditioned. It is often discussed under the heading of role.

One speaks of a gesture, an action, a feeling, a need, a role, an identity, being the complement of a corresponding gesture, action, feeling, need, role, or identity of the other.

A child may grow up to confer a blessing on its parents by fulfilling them in their parenthood. Such complementarity can be genuine or false. Stephen described how his mother was so full of herself that nothing he did seemed to be of any importance to her. Yet, she *needed* him. There was no way that he could be generous, whereas she was always generous. However, he discovered at least one way 'to get at' her: this was to refuse to accept her generosity. Her identity-for-herself depended on establishing collusions with others, to whom she would be the giver while they would be receivers. The receivers were allocated the conflict between envy and gratitude. Already as a child he sensed that herein he could have his revenge for the unwanted position he had been placed in.

Gratifying and being gratified have their dawning origins in breast-feeding. This can be genuinely reciprocal. The baby's need for the breast and the breast's need for the baby coexist from the beginning. The mother receives from the baby, while the baby receives from the mother. The 'good breast' is a breast that can receive as well as give. To take will go along with to give, the act of taking will be simultaneously a giving, and giving will be simultaneously taking.

In these terms, emptiness is not due to an empty stomach. One can feel physically empty when not putting oneself into what one is doing, or when what one is putting oneself into feels intrinsically meaningless to oneself. But emptiness and futility can arise when a person has put himself into his acts, even when these acts seem to have some point to him, if he is accorded no recognition by the other, and if he feels he is not able to make any difference to anyone. It is on this basis, real in imagination or phantasy, that angry destructive attacks in phantasy on a *self-sufficient* 'good' breast are intensified in envy and spite. In phantasy, one destroys what one hates, and hates what one cannot have since one has destroyed it. The unresponsive or impervious other induces a sense of emptiness and impotence in self. Destruction in phantasy of the other sets off a vicious circle. Self receives and gives. Other is needed to give and to receive. The more self receives, the more self needs to give. The more other cannot *receive*, the more self needs to destroy. The more self destroys other, the more empty self becomes. The more empty the more envious, the more envious the more destructive.

A prototype of the other as giver but not receiver, unresponsive or impervious, tends to generate in self a sense of failure. He may be successful in different walks of life, but always feels: 'I've nothing to give really. All I can do is take. Who cares anyway?' He may feel that his life would only have meaning if it made a difference to others, for he feels that this is all that matters: 'to leave your mark'. He may be sexually potent and 'successful', but feel that he never really 'gets through', perpetually frustrated in the midst of gratification. To make a difference to the other is victory. To allow the other to make a difference to him is defeat. Incapable of genuine reciprocity, he never finds it. He fears everyone in case they make a difference to him. If the other gives him love he will spurn it, if he feels that he is given anything; or he will despise it, if he feels the other depends on him to receive anything. Finally, he has lost both sense of his capacity to give and sense of 'the other's' capacity to receive.

Consider this in relation to sex. Two basic intentions in sexuality are pleasurable relief from tension, and change in the other. Sex may be felt to be empty if the other is not dancing as well. The pure self-gratification of rise and fall of tension can be eminently frustrating. Any theory of sexuality which makes the 'aim' of the sexual 'instinct' the achievement of orgasmic potency alone, while the other, however selectively chosen, is a mere object, a means to this end, ignores the erotic desire to make a difference to the other. When Blake suggested that what is most required is 'the lineaments of gratified desire' *in the other,* he indicated that one of the most frustrating possible experiences is full discharge of one's energy or libido, however pleasurable, without making any difference to the other.

Frigidity in women is often the refusal to allow men the triumph of 'giving' satisfaction. Her frigidity is triumph and torment. 'You can have your penis, your erection, your orgasm, but it doesn't make any difference to me.' Indeed erection and orgasm are very limited aspects of potency: potency without power to make a difference to the other. The impotent man, analogously to the frigid women, is often determined not to give the woman the satisfaction of satisfying him.

Jack is potent. Jill is frigid. Jack does not want to ejaculate alone. It means nothing to him. Or rather, he feels he has been rejected. He wants to give her an orgasm. She does not want to be frigid because she would like to give him her orgasm; it would be a present. But if he forces her to have an orgasm it would be a defeat. He would have won and she would have lost. She would, however, like to be defeated, but he does not seem to be able to beat her. Meanwhile if she is not going to come, he is damned if he is, so he now becomes impotent. It usually takes several years of marriage to arrive at this position, but some people can work through the stages in a few months.

Frustration becomes despair when the person begins to question his own capacity to 'mean' anything to anyone.

The prostitute provides the required complementary 'lineaments' for a price. If they are not available in Jill, Jack begins to despair of his power to make any difference to anyone, but may settle for a good counterfeit. Jill may herself be prepared to play the part of the prostitute. It keeps it in the family, as it were.

Every relationship implies a definition of self by other and other by self. This complementarity can be central or peripheral, have greater or less dynamic significance at different periods of one's life. At some point a child rebels against the nexus of bonds which bind him to these parents and siblings whom he has not chosen; he does not wish to be defined and identified as his father's son, or sister's brother. These people may seem strangers to him. Surely, he has affinities with parents who are finer, wiser, more exalted. Yet, this nexus of complementary bonds is an anchor that others long for. Orphans and adopted children sometimes develop a tremendously strong desire to find out 'who they are', by tracing the father and mother who conceived them. They feel incomplete for want of a father or mother, whose absence leaves their concept of self incomplete. Something tangible, even a plaque on a tombstone, may be enough. It seems to allow 'closure'.

A person's 'own' identity cannot be completely abstracted from his identity-for-others. His identity-for-himself; the identity others ascribe to him; the identities he attributes to them; the identity or identities he thinks they attribute to him; what he thinks they think he thinks they think . . .

'Identity' is that whereby one feels one is *the same*, in this place, this time as at that time and at that place, past or future; it is that by which one is identified. I have the impression that most people tend to come to feel that they are the same continuous beings through womb, to tomb. And that this 'identity', the more it is phantasy, is the more intensely defended.

An 'identity' sometimes becomes an 'object' that a person has or feels he has lost, and starts to search for. Many primitive phantasies are attached to identity and 'its' objectification and reification. The frequently described modern search for 'identity' becomes another phantasy scenario.

Intense *frustration* arises from failure to find that other required to establish a satisfactory 'identity'.

Other people become a sort of identity kit, whereby one can piece together a picture of *oneself*. One recognizes *oneself* in that old smile of recognition from that old friend.

Shame, rather than guilt, appears to arise when a person finds himself condemned to an identity as the complement of another he wishes to repudiate, but cannot. It is difficult to establish a consistent identity for oneself – that is, to see oneself consistently in the same way – if definitions of oneself by others are inconsistent or mutually exclusive. The other may define self simultaneously in incompatible ways. Two or more others may identify self simultaneously in compatible ways. To 'fit in with' them all or to repudiate them all may be impossible. Hence mystification, confusion, and conflict.

Contradictory or paradoxical identities, conveyed explicitly or implicitly, by attributions and injunctions or other means (as considered in Chapter 10) may not be recognized as such either by self or by the others. One injunction may be for collusion, although collusion may be impossible. Collusion may consist in not recognizing that there is an injunction for collusion, and not recognizing that the enjoined collusion is not possible. In that case one finds oneself not simply in conflict, but in such confusion that one does not know what the confusion is about and does not know that one does not know that one is confused. Confusion and doubt may be generated by others who offer identities complementary to their identities, feasible if spread out between a number of people but non-compossible as a set *in one* person. Brian could not be his father's son and his mother's son simultaneously (see below). It might have been different had they had two sons. With such an undermined identity he feels driven to try to control all ways he may be defined. Self then repudiates all imposed elements of identity, biological or social. I am who I choose to be. If I choose to be a woman, I *am* a woman. If I choose to be in San Francisco, I am in San Francisco. This 'way out' is usually labelled manic, a mad way out of intolerable dissonances of reciprocally cancelling identities mapped onto self, by self and others.

To 'fit in with' two dissonant definitions at once, what can one do but develop simultaneous incongruities of expression and thereby be each incompatible identity at the one time? Or, without knowing why, one feels suffocated, oppressed, stifled, hemmed in. Or one discovers the manic way out. By snapping one's fingers, one is who, where, and when one chooses, and one can equally make anyone become anyone.

The following two stories illustrate how distracted a person may become even if identity as complementary to others, as this son or daughter of that father and mother, is undermined or *disconfirmed*. Both were in hospital for some months.

BRIAN

At the age of twenty-nine, Brian was admitted to a mental hospital in a state of confusion and despair after being married, apparently happily, for ten years. He had begun to beat his wife brutally with a knotted rope and had taken to drink. He insisted he was wicked 'because there could be no greater wickedness than to inflict gratuitous suffering on a good person who loved you and whom you loved'.

He had lived with his mother until he was four years old. He grew up to believe that his father was dead. His memory of his mother was that she was good, sweet, kind, and innocent. When he was four, he remembers that his mother took him with her on a long journey. They entered a strange house and he met a strange man and woman. His mother burst into tears, kissed him, and ran out. He never saw or heard of her again. The strange man and woman started to call him by his name and told him that they were his mummy and daddy. He remembers that he was confused. This confusion permeated all his feelings, including his grief for his mother. He recollects that his energies went into desperate efforts *to make sense* out of what had happened, rather than into the work of mourning for the loss of his mother. His two 'parents' told him nothing. There were two questions that were truly burning, 'Who is my mummy?' and 'Who am I?' To answer the second, he had to answer the first. In losing his 'old' mother, he lost his 'old' self. The abrupt loss of his identity 'as my mummy's son', and allocation by these two strangers of a new one, 'You are our son', meant: his old mummy had got rid of him because he was bad. This thought was the one thing he had to cling to. It added everything up for him. It became his one certainty. He did not know *who* he was but he did know *what* he was. And if he *was* wicked, then he would *be* wicked.

He remembers that he came to this decision just before his fifth birthday. He could think of nothing terribly bad that he had done, there was nothing he felt terribly sorry about, but he *knew* he was wicked. Because he was wicked he had to do wicked things. Once this identity crystallized, his primary task was to act wickedly.

His two 'parents' had two children of their own, a son, Jack, and a daughter, Betty, respectively eighteen and sixteen years older than he. He was brought up as their younger brother. He remembers that his brother tried to be friends with him, but he was too much enclosed in his own confusion to respond. When he was a little older this brother went to Canada.

He became very naughty and began to be told that he was a bad lot and that he would come to nothing. He was triumphant every time he induced anyone to pass this judgement. At school he tormented a girl who sat beside him who he felt was 'good, sweet, kind, and innocent'. The connection between his 'own' mummy and this girl was apparent to him later, though not at the time. He began to cherish the thought of tormenting in every way any girl or woman who was 'good, sweet, kind, and innocent'. This was the supreme wickedness, and its indulgence in reverie his chief and very secret delight.

When he was nine a decisive event occurred. Without his 'parents'' knowledge, he discovered his own adoption papers and learnt that he was not one of 'them'. He concealed this knowledge from everyone and became full of contempt and scorn for his 'adoptive' parents. The petty hypocrisy, deceit, and cowardice of these people who expected him to 'fall for' their stories that he was one of 'them' just because they said so! Every time he was naughty and they said in anger that he would come to nothing, he endorsed his conviction that their 'love' for him was simply hypocrisy and that he really meant nothing to them. 'They simply got a boy instead of a dog for their old age.' But he thought 'I will play their game for the time being.' Open wickedness would simply play into their hands.

By the age of eight he had come to believe that they were trying to drive him to be bad by telling him he was. He felt if he came to a bad end he would simply be giving them satisfaction. If he was a future nobody, the best way to frustrate, spite, and torment them was to become a somebody. Accordingly his phase of being a difficult 'psychopathic' child ended and he began to do well at lessons and to be well behaved generally, thereby calling his 'parents'' bluff by forcing them into hypocritical expressions of pleasure at his achievements. By his teens he had elaborated intricate levels of deception. At sixteen his parents broke the news that he was adopted, under the impression that he believed himself to be a member of their family and had forgotten his mummy. He pretended to be shattered by this revelation, while secretly full of hatred and contempt for these fools who thought they could drive him to the gallows that easily.

On leaving school, he went into business. Pushed on by revenge and spite to become somebody, he became a successful business man.

After tormenting the little girl at school, he had not acted upon his reveries and dreams of tormenting girls. He regarded himself as quiet, diffident, and charming towards woman. In due course, in his early twenties, he married the girl of his reveries and dreams, a girl who was 'good, sweet, kind, and innocent'. Their marriage was happy and they had a son. Then he began to quarrel with his wife compulsively and un-justifiably. He drank heavily. He acquired a large, heavy rope. He knotted it and beat her with it until she ran to her parents in terror and bewilderment. Their son was four years old.

He had driven his wife away when their son was the same age as he had been when his mother left him. His son's approach to this age evoked his original crisis when he lost his original identity along with his mother. To repeat: His mother did not simply go away. That woman who went away was *not* his mother. So who was he who was left?

His drinking and attacks on his wife revealed his long-concealed phantasy infrastructure, which he had concealed so well that even he had become unaware of it. The reality co-efficient, as it were, of his wife's identity as a person suddenly fell.

To the two catastrophic events – the loss of his old identity, the discovery that his new identity was false – another must be added. This may have been the final precipitating factor, as one says. Just before his 'disturbed behaviour' began, he had returned to his 'home' at Christmas. Much of his bitterness had left him. He had discovered, as he felt, genuine happiness with his wife for the first time in his life. After those many years he had at last come to terms with the fact that he was adopted:

that he did not 'belong'. He could 'understand' that his 'parents' had 'thought it best' to deceive him. When at 'home' he had a talk with his sister and was able to tell for the first time a little about the feelings he kept secret all his life. He would always regret, however, that he would never know who his father was.

'But didn't you know?' she said, 'I thought my parents had told you. Jack was your father.'

Jack, the 'brother' who had made a special effort to be 'friends' with him when his mother had left him with the family, had recently died in Canada. This was one too many turns of the screw. It was 'beyond a joke'. His most prized secret possession had been that he *knew* he was not 'one of them'. The structure of the meaning of his life was destroyed. *He* was torn to shreds. He had been fooled completely. Unsuspectingly, he had grown up where in fact he had belonged. The stupidity, the senselessness of it! He reverted to a certainty which no one could take from him. He would make certain that he *was* bad. He was wicked. He would remove the last possibilities of doubt on that score. He drank himself stupid and flogged his wife until she left him and he had to be taken away.

When his wife did leave him he only half realized that he had driven her to this. He was also taken aback. He had nourished the idea that his wife was so totally 'good, sweet, kind, and innocent' that she would never leave him, no matter how bad he was, no matter what he did. He had kept in and by him a 'mother' who endured torture without complaining, punishing, or leaving him. He fused his 'mother' with his wife. When she left him, she showed that *she* was bad as well as himself because she did not love him unconditionally. He devised a way he could have final revenge, the final solution whereby at one and the same time he could 'pay her off' and bind her to him for ever. He would kill himself, so that she would inherit his money. She would then never be able to leave him, because she would never be able to forgive herself.

Brian's life seems almost diabolically contrived for comical effects. His story is exceptional, but just for this reason we may be able to see some general truths with particular clarity.

It is difficult to predict what identity a man will embrace. It might be called pivotal, when his whole hierarchy of intentions and projects, whom and what he loves, hates, and fears, his sense of success or failure, pivot around it. It may only be through some apparently insignificant event that its pivoted character comes to light.

Something happens that is incompatible with this pivotal identity, perhaps hidden, that determines his whole system of meaning. A linch-pin is removed that had been holding a whole world together. The whole meaning of reality crumbles. It 'takes the ground from under his feet'. Participation in the world, such terms as 'contact with' and 'sense of reality', are empty sounds. A desperate crisis indeed. Either one restructures one's whole 'real' view of others and the world and redefines one's 'real' self; or one annuls the chasm between what is the case and what one *knows* to be the case, by taking one's stand on what one *knows*. There is nothing more real and indubitable than pure phantasy; nothing more obvious; nothing less necessary and more easy to prove.

One's self-identity is the story one tells one's self of who one is. One's need to believe this story often seems to be one's desire to discount another story, that is more primitive and more terrible. The need to pivot one's life around a complementary identity (i.e. I am my father's son, husband's wife) betokens a dread of phantasy and hatred of what is.

Jesus spoke of leaving one's parents. Did he mean, among other things, that one is not wise to cling for ultimate security to *their* system of reference, that not this way does one find oneself.

The sense Brian made of his sudden, inexplicable abandonment by his mother was: *because* I am bad. To be bad was his credo. He lived by it. It was the rock on which he built his life. 'Since I am bad, there is nothing but to *be* bad.' At the age of eight he confirmed his demonic hatred and contempt by seeming good, sweet, kind, innocent, and successful. Being bad by seeming to be good was simply another revolution round his world-pole. The central pivot remained unchanged. He 'knew' he was *not* their child. He 'knew' he was bad basically. He 'knew' that they did not know that he 'knew' the truth. On this he continued to base himself. His sister's words: 'Didn't you know that Jack was your father?' had the effect of removing the linch-pin that was keeping his whole world in place. When his illusory disillusion was shattered, the straw he clutched as he whistled into the empty vortex was: 'I am bad.' And now: 'I had forgotten for a little while, but I'll make up for it.'

In phantasy the identity 'I am bad' is not so much a complementary identity, but an identity by introjective identification, the fusion of himself with a 'bad mother'. Attacks on his wife involved attacks 'in phantasy' upon both the re-projection of this 'bad mother' and the projection of his own 'innocence'. They were *felt* by him to be expressions of sheer badness directed at sheer goodness. He was submerged in phantasy, *hence* he could not see it as such. It was 'unconscious'. He confused, in and between himself and his wife, his utterly good and utterly bad mother. His complete unconsciousness of this is an index to me that, since his mother left him, he had lost himself and had never rediscovered himself, although looked at from outside he was perfectly normal until this 'illusion' suddenly came on 'out of the blue'.

The others tell one who one is. Later one endorses, or tries to discard, the ways the others have defined one. It is difficult not to accept their story. One may try not to be what one 'knows' one is, in one's heart of hearts. One may try to tear out from oneself this 'alien' identity one has been endowed with or condemned to, and create by one's own actions an identity for oneself, which one tries to force others to confirm. Whatever its particular subsequent vicissitudes, however, one's first social identity is conferred on one. We learn to be whom we are told we are.

When one has no knowledge of one's real parents, or if one grows up to discover that the people one thought were one's 'real' parents are not, one's problem is whether to feel deprived of this identity, or lucky to have escaped it. Frequently such people feel it to be a compelling issue to discover their parents, especially their mother. There are many motives, revenge and hate among them, but there always seems to be the assumption that through establishing one's biological origin one will really know who one really is. Or at least the negative: if one does not know one's parents, one cannot know oneself. One man said, 'I am a book with no beginning. . . .' Yet the quest to discover who one's parents were, however understandable, cannot in itself lead one to oneself.

The 'family romance' is a dream of changing the others who define the self, so that *the identity of the self can be self-defined* by a re-definition of the others. It is an attempt to feel pride rather than shame at being the son or daughter of this father and this mother.

JOHN

John was the son of a prostitute and a naval officer. He lived with his mother until he was six, when he was transferred to his father's care. He was transported into a completely different world. His father, who had not married, sent him to a public school where he did well until, unexpectedly, he failed his university entrance exam. Thereupon he was drafted into the Navy, but failed to become an officer. His father, who was a very exacting man, had been somewhat upset by his son's failure at university level, but was much more upset by his failure to become an officer, and it drew from him the remark that he did not think he could be his son at all. When, in the next few months, John disgraced himself as a sailor in a number of ways, his father told him plainly that he was not his son any more, and that he now knew he never had been. He formally disowned him.

During his early months in the Navy, John was noted to get into states of anxiety, and it was on the grounds of anxiety neurosis that he had been turned down as an officer. Subsequently, however, his behaviour earned the label of psychopathic delinquent, and it was out of keeping with his 'character' hitherto. When his father disowned him his deviance escalated to what was called an acute manic psychosis. His basic premise had become: *he could be anyone he wanted, merely by snapping his fingers*.

His father's method of punishment had been to destroy his identity as his son. He succeeded. Being 'disowned' was a sword of Damocles that finally fell on him. Instead of growing up with the feeling, 'I am my father's son no matter what I do, and whether he or I like it or not', he grew up feeling: 'Only if I succeed in doing certain things will I be my father's son'. *He had* to *prove* he was. Without any other firm ground, he based himself on what *we* are pleased to call a *delusion*, that he could be who he wanted. However, his father's premise only looks more sane superficially.

What his father taught him was: 'You are my son if I say you are, and you are not my son if I say you are not.' He replaced this by: 'I am who *I* say I am, and I am not who *I* say I am not.'

When he became manic, he had not yet quite come to understand how close he was to the truth. But he was one step nearer the truth in his mania than he had been before. He had yet to understand the false position he was placed in by his father, which had become untenable. When he was able to realize that he was not who his father said he was or was not, he stopped counterfeiting this realization by deluding himself. He realized that he was deceiving himself in exactly the same way as his father deceived him.

The root error of his psychosis was in the soil of his pre-psychotic assumptions. His psychosis seemed to be not so much a *reductio ad absurdum* of these assumptions, as a conjuring with the absurdity already present. Namely, that he was who his father said he was. He negated this by: 'No, I am who I say I am.' True sanity lies at the other side: the negation of the psychotic negation of the false original premise. I am not what they say I am, nor what I say I am.

Binswanger has called mania a swindle. In a sense it is a doublecross. One has been tricked out of one's heritage by being told one is a beggar, so one tricks oneself back by pretending one is not really a beggar but really a prince. Fortunately the others do not believe it either.

CHAPTER 7

Confirmation and Disconfirmation

In human society, at all its levels, persons confirm one another in a practical way, to some extent or other, in their personal qualities and capacities, and a society may be termed human in the measure to which its members confirm one another.

The basis of man's life with man is twofold, and it is one – the wish of every man to be confirmed as what he is, even as what he can become, by men; and the innate capacity in man to confirm his fellow-men in this way. That this capacity lies so immeasurably fallow constitutes the real weakness and questionableness of the human race: actual humanity exists only where this capacity unfolds. On the other hand, of course, an empty claim for confirmation, without devotion for being and becoming, again and again mars the truth of the life between man and man.

Men need, and it is granted to them, to confirm one another in their individual being by means of genuine meetings: but beyond this they need, and it is granted to them, to see the truth, which the soul gains by its struggle, light up to the others, the brothers, in a different way, and even so be confirmed.

MARTIN BUBER (1957a)

TOTAL confirmation of one man by another is an ideal possibility seldom realized. For practical purposes, as Buber states, confirmation is always 'to some extent or other'. Any human interaction implies some measure of confirmation, at any rate of the physical bodies of the participants, even when one person is shooting another. The slightest sign of recognition from another at least confirms one's presence in *his* world. 'No more fiendish punishment could be devised,' William James once wrote, 'even were such a thing physically possible, than that one should be turned loose in society and remain absolutely unnoticed by all the members thereof.'

Thus, we can think of confirmation as partial and varying in manner, as well as global and absolute. One can think of action and interaction sequences as more or less, and in different ways, *confirmatory* or *disconfirmatory*. Confirmation can vary in intensity and extensity, quality and quantity. By reacting 'lukewarmly', imperviously, tangentially, and so on, one fails to endorse some aspects of the other, while endorsing other aspects.

Modes of confirmation or disconfirmation vary. Confirmation could be through a responsive smile (visual), a handshake (tactile), an expression of sympathy (auditory). A confirmatory response is *relevant* to the evocative action, it accords recognition to the evocatory act, and accepts its significance for the evoker, if not for the respondent. A confirmatory reaction is a direct response, it is 'to the point', or 'on the same wavelength' as the initiatory or evocatory action. A partially confirmatory response need not be in agreement, or gratifying, or satisfying. Rejection can be confirmatory if it is direct, not tangential, and recognizes the evoking action and grants it significance and validity.

There are different levels of confirmation or disconfirmation. An action may be confirmed at one level and disconfirmed at another. Some forms of 'rejection' imply limited recognition – the perception of and responsiveness to what is rejected. An action 'rejected' is perceived and this perception shows that it is accepted as a fact. Direct 'rejection' is not tangential; it is not mocking or in other ways invalidating. It need neither depreciate nor exaggerate the original action. It is not synonymous with indifference or imperviousness.

Some areas of a person's being may cry out for confirmation more than others. Some forms of disconfirmation may be more destructive of self-development than others. One may call these schizogenic. The ontogenesis of confirmation and disconfirmation has barely begun to be explored. Responsiveness adequate to the infant will be inappropriate to an older child or an adult. There may be periods in one's life when one has experienced more confirmation or disconfirmation than at other periods. The qualities and capacities confirmed or disconfirmed by mother or father, brothers, sisters, friends, may differ widely. An aspect of oneself negated by one person may be endorsed by another. A part or aspect of oneself which is 'false', or which one regards as false, may be confirmed actively and persistently by one or both parents, or even by all the significant others at the same time. At different periods of life, the practical or felt need for, and modes of, confirmation or disconfirmation vary, both as to the aspects of the person's being in question and as to the modes of confirming or disconfirming particular aspects.

Many families have now been studied (not only those in which one person has come to be regarded as psychotic) where there is little genuine confirmation of the parents by each other and of the child by each parent, separately or together, but this may not be obvious, though it can be studied objectively. One finds interactions marked by pseudo-confirmation, by acts which masquerade as confirming but are counterfeit.[1] Pretences at confirmation go through the appearances of confirmation. The absence of genuine confirmation, or pseudo-confirmation, may take the form of confirming a fiction the child is taken to be, without the actual child receiving recognition. The characteristic family pattern that has emerged from the studies of the families of schizophrenics does not so much involve a child who is subject to outright neglect or even to obvious trauma, but a child who has been subjected to subtle but persistent disconfirmation, usually unwittingly. For many years lack of genuine confirmation takes

1. Cf. Wynne *et al.* (1958).

the form of actively confirming a false self, so that the person whose false self is confirmed and real self disconfirmed is placed in a false position. Someone in a false position *feels guilt, shame, or anxiety at not being false*. Confirmation of a false self goes on without anyone in the family being aware that this is the state of affairs. The schizogenic potential of the situation seems to reside largely in the fact that it is not recognized by anyone; or if the mother or father or some other member or friend of the family is aware of this state of affairs, it is not brought into the open and no effort is made to intervene – if such intervention were only to state the truth of the matter.

Here we shall look at some acts of confirmation or disconfirmation, without prejudgements as to whether or to what extent they are schizogenic.

There may be a failure to recognize a person as agent. The attribution of agency to human beings is one way we distinguish people from things set in motion by agents external to themselves. In some childhoods this quality of being human, whereby one can come to feel that one is an agent in one's own right, is not confirmed by the original significant others. It is illuminating to match observations on the way a child is treated by his parents with the 'delusions' the psychotic child or adult expresses.

Julie said she was a 'tolled bell' (told belle), that she was 'tailored bread' (bred). When it was possible to observe the interaction between her mother and her, one could see that her mother could not or did not confirm agency on Julie's part. Her mother could not respond to spontaneity and *inter*acted with her only if she, mother, could initiate the interaction. Her mother visited the hospital daily. One saw Julie daily sitting passively while her mother combed her hair, put ribbons and hairpins in it, powdered her face, applied lipstick to her lips and mascara to her eyes, so that the final appearance resembled nothing so much as that of a beautiful, lifesize, lifeless doll which her mother 'told' (tolled). Julie seemed to have been her mother's 'transitional object', to use Winnicott's term. One might say: 'What could her mother do but this, if her daughter was catatonic?' It is significant and remarkable that it was *this passive listless 'thing' which her mother regarded as normal*. She reacted to spontaneity on Julie's part with anxiety and attributions of badness or madness. To be good was to do what she was told (Laing, 1960, pp. 196–224).

FURTHER EXAMPLES OF CONFIRMATION AND DISCONFIRMATION

1. During direct observation of the relationship between a six-month-old child and its mother, the occasions in which smiling occurred were noted. It was observed, first of all, that infant and mother smiled at each other not infrequently. It was then further observed that the mother, during the periods of observation, never once responded with a smile to the infant's initial smile at her. She, however, evoked smiling in the infant by smiling herself, by tickling and playing with the infant. When she was the evoker of the infant's smiles, she in turn smiled back, but she responded with a flat, dull look if the infant took the initiative (cf. Brodey, 1959).

2. A little boy of five runs to his mother holding a big fat worm in his hand, and says, 'Mummy, look what a big fat worm I have got.' She says, 'You are filthy – away and clean yourself immediately.' The mother's response to the boy is an example of what Ruesch (1958) has called a *tangential response*.

Ruesch writes:

The criteria which characterize the tangential responses can be summarized as follows:

The reply inadequately fits the initial statement.

The reply has a frustrating effect.

The reply is not geared to the intention behind the original state-ment as it is perceivable through word, action, and context of the situation. The reply emphasizes an aspect of the statement which is incidental (Ruesch, op. cit., pp. 37–48).

In terms of the boy's feeling, the mother's response is at a tangent, as it were. She does not say, 'Oh yes, what a lovely worm.' She does not say, 'What a filthy worm – you mustn't touch worms like that; throw it away.' She does not express pleasure or horror, approval or disapproval of the worm, but she responds by focusing on something which he has not considered and which has no immediate importance to him, namely whether he is clean or dirty. She may be saying either, 'I am not interested in looking at your worm unless you are clean', or, 'Whether or not you have a worm is of no im-portance to me – all that matters to me is whether you are clean or dirty, and I only like you when you are clean.' In developmental terms, the mother can be seen as ignoring the genital level in the boy symbolized by the big fat worm, and as recognizing only the anal issue of clean or dirty.

In this tangential response there is a failure to endorse what the boy is *doing* from his point of view, namely, showing his mummy a worm. 'Boy with worm' is an identity that might facilitate a later identity of 'man with penis'. Persistent ab-sence of a confirmatory response to boy-with-worm may lead the boy to make some detours before he can arrive at being a man with a penis. He might decide to collect worms. He might feel that he can collect worms only if he keeps him-self very clean. He might feel that he can collect worms as long as his mother knows nothing about it. He might feel that the most important thing was to be clean and have his mother's approval, and that collecting worms did not matter. He might develop a phobia for worms. At all events, one imagines that, although his mother has not openly disapproved of his having a worm, her indifference to it is likely to generate at least some transitory confusion, anxiety, and guilt in him, and that if this particular response epitomizes the exchanges between him and his mother at this stage in his development, then it is going to be that much more difficult for him to have an unselfconscious, guilt-and-anxiety-free, non-defiant, real sense of the many aspects of being 'boy-with-worm' and 'man-with penis'.

Furthermore, since the issues in terms of which his mother perceives him are clean–dirty, good–bad, and her equations are clean = good, dirty = bad, he will at some point have to decide whether these are the decisive issues and the necessary equations for him. If he is dirty, he may get to the point that, although his mother told him he was bad, he does not feel bad; and, conversely, that if he is clean he is not necessarily good: that he might well be good yet dirty, or bad yet clean. Or even no longer live by puzzling out the matrix of good–dirty–bad–clean. He may come to identify himself through these issues and equations, to become a good–clean or a bad–dirty boy and man, and ignore as tangential to his real concerns all those aspects of his life which do not fit these categories.

3. I began a session with a schizophrenic woman of twenty-five, who sat down in a chair some distance away from me while I sat half facing her in another chair. After about ten minutes during which she had not moved or spoken, my mind began to drift away on preoccupations of my own. In the midst of these, I heard her say in a very small voice, 'Oh please don't go so far away from me.'

Psychotherapy with real card-carrying schizophrenics is a separate subject, but the following are a few remarks on the issue of confirmation or disconfirmation in psychotherapy.

When she made this remark I could have responded in many ways. A comment some psychotherapists might make is, 'You feel I am away from you.' By this, one would neither confirm nor disconfirm the validity of her 'feeling' that I was no longer 'with' her, but would confirm the fact that she experienced me as away. The endorsement of the 'feeling' is noncommittal about the validity of the feeling, namely, whether or not *I* was actually going away from her. One could 'interpret' why she should be frightened at me not staying 'with' her, e.g. a need to have me 'with' her as a defence against her own anger if I am not. One might construe her plea as an expression of her need to fill her emptiness by my presence, or to treat me as a 'transitional object', and so on.

In my view the most important thing for me to do at that moment was to confirm the fact that she had correctly registered *my* actual withdrawal of my 'presence'. There are many patients who are very sensitive to desertion, but are not sure of the reliability, much less validity, of their own sensitivity. They do not trust other people, and they cannot trust their own mistrust either. Jill is tormented, for instance, by not knowing whether she just 'feels' that Jack is preoccupied and uninterested, while Jack is pretending to be intensely attentive; or whether she can 'trust' her feelings to register the real state of the relationship. One of the most important questions, therefore, is whether such mistrust of her 'feelings' and the testimony of others arises from persistent inconsistencies within an original nexus – between the evidence of empathic attributions about others, her experience of herself, the testimony of others about their feelings, and the constructions they place on her experience of, and intentions towards, them, etc. – so that she has never been able to arrive at any trust in herself in any respect.

The only thing, therefore, I could say to my patient was, 'I am sorry.'

4. A nurse was engaged to look after a somewhat catatonic, hebephrenic schizophrenic patient. Shortly after they had met, the nurse gave the patient a cup of tea. This chronically psychotic patient, on taking the tea, said, 'This is the first time in my life that anyone has ever given me a cup of tea.' Subsequent experience with this patient tended to substantiate the simple truth of this statement.[2]

It is not so easy for one person to give another a cup of tea. If a lady gives me a cup of tea, she might be showing off her teapot, or her tea-set; she might be trying to put me in a good mood in order to get something out of me; she may be trying to get me to like her; she may be wanting me as an ally for her own purposes against others. She might pour tea from a teapot into a cup and shove out her hand with cup and saucer in it, whereupon I am expected to grab them within the two seconds before they will become a dead weight. The action could be a mechanical one in which there is no recognition of *me* in it. A cup of tea could be handed me without *me* being *given* a *cup of tea*.

In our tea ceremonial, it is the simplest and most difficult thing in the world for *one person*, genuinely being his or her self, *to give*, in fact and not just in appearance, *another person*, realized in his or her own being by the giver, *a cup of tea*, really, and not in appearance. This patient is saying that many cups of tea have passed from other hands to hers in the course of her life, but this notwithstanding, she has never in her life had a cup of tea really given her.

Some people are more sensitive than others to not being recognized as human beings. If someone is *very* sensitive in this respect, they stand a good chance of being diagnosed as schizophrenic. Freud said of hysterics, as Fromm-Reichmann was later to say of schizophrenics, that they needed both to give and receive more love than most people. One could put

2. This anecdote was told me by Dr Charles Rycroft.

this the other way round. If you need to give and receive *too much* 'love',[3] you will be a high risk for the diagnosis of schizophrenia. This diagnosis attributes to you the incapacity, by and large, to give or receive 'love' in an adult manner. When you smile at such a thought, this may confirm the diagnosis since you are suffering from 'inappropriate effect'.

3. Whatever 'love' is.

CHAPTER 8

Collusion

THE term 'collusion' has kinship with de-lusion, il-lusion, and
e-lusion. Lusion comes from the verb *ludere,* whose meaning
varies in classical and late Latin. It can mean to play, to play at,
or to make a sport of, to mock, to deceive.

Delusion implies total self-deception. Illusion, as frequently
used psychoanalytically, implies a capacity to deceive oneself
under a strong wish, but does not involve self-deception as
total as delusion.

Collusion has resonances of playing at and of deception. It
is a 'game' played by two or more people whereby they
deceive themselves. The game *is* the game of mutual self-
deception. Whereas delusion and elusion and illusion can be
applied to one person, collusion is necessarily a two-or-more-
person game. Each plays the other's game, though he may not
necessarily be fully aware of doing so. An essential feature of
this game is not admitting that it is a game. When the one
person is predominantly the passive 'victim' (one can be
victimized for not playing 'victim') of a trick or manoeuvre or
manipulation, the relationship will not be called collusive. It
will be difficult in practice to determine whether or to what
extent a relationship is collusive. But the distinction is still
worth making in theory. A slave may collude with his master
in being a slave to save his life, even to the point of carrying
out orders that are self-destructive.

Two people in relation may confirm each other or genuinely
complement each other. Still, to disclose oneself to the other is
hard without confidence in oneself and trust in the other.
Desire for confirmation from each is present in both, but each

is caught between trust and mistrust, confidence and despair, and both settle for counterfeit acts of confirmation on the basis of pretence. To do so *both* must play the game of collusion.

Buber (1957b) asks us to

... imagine two men, whose life is dominated by appearances, sitting and talking together. Call them Peter [p] and Paul [o].[1] Let us list the different configurations which are involved. First, there is Peter as he wishes to appear to Paul [$p \rightarrow (o \rightarrow p)$] and Paul as he wishes to appear to Peter [$o \rightarrow (p \rightarrow o)$]. Then there is Peter as he really appears to Paul, that is Paul's image of Peter [$o \rightarrow p: p \rightarrow (o \rightarrow p)$], which in general does not in the least coincide with what Peter wishes Paul to see; and similarly there is the reverse situation [$p \rightarrow o: o \rightarrow (p \rightarrow o)$]. Further, there is Peter as he appears to himself [$p \rightarrow p$], and Paul as he appears to himself [$o \rightarrow o$]. Lastly, there are the bodily Peter and the bodily Paul, two living beings and six ghostly appearances, which mingle in many ways in the conversations between the two. Where is there room for any genuine inter-human life?

Consider this relation as a game of counterfeiting a relation. Peter or Paul may try to establish an identity for himself by achieving a particular identity for the other. Peter finds it necessary for Paul to see him in a particular light, in order for him, Peter, to feel that he is the person he wants to be. Peter needs Paul to be a certain person in order for Peter to be the person he wishes to be. For Peter to experience himself as seen in this light, Paul has to see him in this light. If Peter needs to be appreciated, then Paul has to be seen to appreciate him. If Paul is seen not to appreciate him, Peter is motivated to make out that Paul is not able to do so. If it is necessary for Peter to be generous, Paul must accept Peter's generosity. If Paul, instead of being grateful to Peter for what Peter gives him,

---

1. The notation within square brackets is mine (see Appendix).

says that Peter is simply wishing to show his own superiority by being a person who can give, or by saying that he is trying to blackmail Paul into being grateful to him, Peter may break off the relationship with Paul or discover that Paul has difficulties in allowing himself to be helped. Peter may be seen by Paul or Paul may be seen by Peter in more real terms than either can see himself. The need for such appearances arises from phantasies of each. The need for appearances implies not that both are hiding their 'true' selves, which they secretly know, but that neither has Peter arrived at any genuine realization of himself or of Paul, nor has Paul any genuine realization of himself or of Peter.

There are many reactions, so far relatively unexplored systematically by interpersonal psychology, to being seen by the other not as one sees oneself. Where there is disjunction between Peter's self-identity, $p \rightarrow p$, and his identity-for-Paul, $o \rightarrow p$, one is not surprised if Peter reacts with anger, anxiety, guilt, despair, indifference. A disjunction of this kind lends fuel to some relationships. It seems the cement, almost, that binds some people together. In this bondage, it is 'the issue' they compulsively take up with each other again and again. Alternatively, some people in this disjunction abandon the relationship.

The issue is related to the situation when there are incompatibilities between the 'complement' that Peter may wish to be to Paul and the 'complement' that Paul may wish to be to Peter. A man wishes his wife to 'mother' him, while she wishes him to mother her. Their wishes do not 'fit' or dovetail. They hate each other or despise each other, or tolerate the other's weakness, or they recognize the other's need without fulfilling it. However, if Jack insists on seeing and acting towards Jill as his mother, while impervious to the fact that she feels like a little girl in relation to her mother, the disjunction between his concept of her and her experience of herself may open out a chasm of incompatibility that collusion cannot bridge.

This is something other than what is meant by the psychoanalytic term 'projection'. The one person does not use the other merely as a hook to hang projections on. He strives to find in the other, or to induce the other to become, the very *embodiment* of projection. The other person's collusion is required to 'complement' the identity self feels impelled to sustain. One can experience a peculiar form of guilt, specific, I think, to this disjunction. If one refuses collusion, one feels guilt for not being or not becoming the embodiment of the complement demanded by the other for his identity. However if one *does* succumb, if one is seduced, one becomes estranged from one's self and is guilty thereby of self-betrayal.

If one does not take fright at experiencing oneself as engulfed by the other, resent being 'used', or in some way rebel against collusion, then under pressure from a false guilt one may become, as one may feel, the unwilling accomplice or victim of the other, although being 'the victim' may be also an act of collusion. But the other may induce self to assume that false self that hankers to be and that he may embody only too gladly, especially if other reciprocates by embodying a fiction that self desires. We shall leave for a moment more detailed considerations of forms and techniques of open or concealed, consistent or incompatible, appeals or coercions that one person can make to another, and the widely different ways that other may experience and react to them.

Collusion is always clinched when self finds in other that other who will 'confirm' self in the false self that is trying to make real, and vice versa. The ground is then set for prolonged mutual evasion of truth and true fulfilment. Each has found an other to endorse his own false notion of himself and to give this appearance a semblance of reality.

A third party is always a danger to a two-person collusion.

With a geometrical precision reminiscent of Spinoza, Sartre's *Huis Clos* (1946) depicts an infernal round of collusive two-somes in impossible trials. *Huis Clos* reveals the agony of failure to sustain identity when the project of one's life is such that a tolerable self-identity requires collusion. Three dead people, a man and two women, find themselves in a room together. The man is a coward; one woman is a heterosexual bitch, the other a clever lesbian. The man fears he is a coward, and that other men will not respect him. The heterosexual woman fears that she is not attractive to men. The lesbian fears that women will not be attracted to her. The man needs another man or, second best, an intelligent woman to see him as brave so that he can deceive himself that he is brave. He is prepared as far as he can to be what either of the two women want him to be, if only they will collude with him by telling him that he is brave. However, the one woman can only see him as a sexual object. He cannot give the lesbian anything she wants, except to be a coward, for this is how she requires to see men to justify herself. The two women cannot form a stable collusion with anyone, the lesbian since she is with a man and a heterosexual woman, the heterosexual woman since she cannot *be* a heterosexual woman without 'meaning' something to a man. But this man is not interested. Each cannot sustain his 'bad faith' without collusion with another, each remains tormented and haunted by anxiety and despair. In this situation, '*l'enfer, c'est les autres*'.

Genet (1957b) in his play *The Balcony*, has taken the theme of fake relationships based on collusive and complementary con-junctions of identity-for-self and identity-for-the-other. Most of the play takes place in a brothel. The girls in the brothel are shown to be, in a literal sense, pro-stitutes. They stand for (*pro-stare*) whatever the client requires them to be, so that he can become for a while who he wishes to be. Three such identities for which colluding prostitutes are required are

Bishop, Judge, General. The Bishop requires a penitent to condemn and an executioner to carry out his orders; the Judge, a thief; the General, his mare.

As the Judge explains to the girl who must be a thief for him to be a judge: 'You have got to be a model thief if I am to be a model judge. If you are a fake thief, I become a fake judge. Is that clear?'

He says to the executioner: '... without you, I would be nothing....' And then to the thief: '... and without you too, my child. You are my two perfect complements. Ah, what a fine trio we make!'

To the thief (p. 18):

THE JUDGE: But you, you have a privilege that he hasn't, nor I either, that of priority. My being a judge is an emanation of your being a thief. You need only refuse – but you'd better not! – need only refuse to be who you are – what you are, therefore who you are – for me to cease to be ... to vanish evaporated. Burst. Volatised. Denied. Hence good born of ... What then? What then? But you won't refuse, will you? You won't refuse to be a thief! That would be wicked. It would be criminal You'd deprive me of being! [*imploringly*] Say it, my child, my love, you won't refuse?

THE THIEF: [*coyly*] I might.

THE JUDGE: What's that? What's that you say? You'd refuse? Tell me where. And tell me again what you've stolen.

THE THIEF: [*Curtly, and getting up*] I won't.

THE JUDGE: Tell me where. Don't be cruel ...

THE THIEF: Your tone is getting too familiar. I won't have it!

THE JUDGE: Miss ... Madame. I beg of you. [*He falls to his knees.*] Look, I beseech you. Don't leave me in this position, waiting to be a judge. If there were no judge, what would become of us, but what if there were no thieves?

People use the brothel in order to make what singly could only be an *illusionary* or *delusionary identity* into a *collusive identity*. Madame lists the 'identities' for which her clients patronize the brothel.

There are two kings of France with coronation ceremonies and different rituals, an admiral at the stern of his sinking destroyer, a bishop during the perpetual adoration, a judge performing his functions, a general on horseback, a boy of Algiers surrendering, a fireman putting out a fire, a goat attached to a stake, a housewife returning from market, a pickpocket, a robbed man who's bound and beaten up, a Saint Sebastian, a farmer in his barn ... but no chief of police ... nor colonial administrator, though there *is* a missionary dying on the cross, and Christ in person (p. 46).

One person does not visit the brothel to become somebody else – the Chief of Police. He feels the fulfilment of his life would be when another wishes to assume *his* identity, to become the Chief of Police. He suffers because no one wants to play at being him, for in the history of the brothel his is the one identity for which there has been no client. All human beings are his complements. This no longer satisfies him. He alone does not wish to assume the identity of another. He will be fulfilled, and therefore able to die, only when another identifies with him.

The brothel is challenged by the Revolution. The Revolution to end illusion and collusion. The Revolution to become oneself, to be serious, to be what one is. One of the girls from the brothel has escaped to become the mistress of Roger, the leader of the Revolution. But her vocation is to be a prostitute. She has not the knack of simply doing what she is doing. She is unable to perform an act for its own sake. If she is dressing a wound, she cannot but play at dressing a wound, whether it be with tender solicitude or whether it be roughly and matter-of-factly. The leaders of the Revolution recognize that the people need to be inspired to fight and to die. They need an emblem. They cannot sustain their revolt without illusion. They decide to use Chantal, the girl from the brothel, who is born to embody the illusions of men; she is a born symbol. Roger opposes this use of Chantal on principle, but he is overruled. A member of the Revolutionary Committee addresses him:

LUKE: I'm not impressed by your speeches. I still maintain that in certain cases you've got to use the enemy's weapons. That it's indispensable. Enthusiasm for freedom? It's a fine thing, I don't deny it, but it would be even finer if freedom were a pretty girl with a warm voice. After all, what does it matter to you if we storm the barricades by following a female like a pack of males in heat? And what of it if the groans of the dying are the groans of life?

ROGER: Men don't revolt in order to go chasing after a female.

LUKE: [*stubbornly*] Even if the chase leads them to victory?

ROGER: Then their victory is already sick. Their victory has a dose of clap, to talk like you ... (p. 57).

Chantal embodies what Roger wishes to destroy. Yet he loves in her what made it possible for her to enter the brothel, and her incapacity not to symbolize and embody what men die for.

CHANTAL: The brothel has at least been of some use to me, for it has taught me the art of shamming and acting. I've had to play so many roles that I know almost all of them. And I've had so many partners ... (p. 64).

Chantal's capacity is too compelling for the revolutionary leaders not to try to turn it to their account, and thereby destroy their own Revolution.

MARK: We're going to use Chantal. Her job's to embody the Revolution. The job of the mothers and the widows is to mourn the dead. The job of the dead is to cry for revenge. The job of our heroes is to die with a smile. .... The Palace will be occupied this evening. From the balcony of the Palace Chantal will rouse the people, and sing. The time for reasoning is past; now's the time to get steamed up and fight like mad. Chantal embodies the struggle; the people are waiting for her to represent victory.

ROGER: And when we're victors, what'll we have gained?

MARK: There'll be time enough to think of that (p. 63).

The seriousness of the Revolution is turning to song and carnival. The Queen's envoy, who is in close liaison with the brothel, says:

I don't doubt their courage or cleverness, but my spies are in the thick of the revolution, and in some cases they're rebels themselves. Now, the populace, which is intoxicated with its first victories, has reached the point of exaltation at which one light-heartedly forsakes actual combat for useless sacrifice. It will be easy to take the leap. The peoples are not engaging in battle. They're indulging in revelry (p. 71).

The Revolution, nevertheless, seems to be at the point of carrying the day, since the Queen, Bishop, Judge, and General have been killed or have disappeared, if they ever existed. But the envoy from the Queen persuades the Madame to dress up as the Queen, and three clients to dress up as Bishop, Judge, and General. They appear so attired at the balcony of the brothel. They drive through the city. They are photographed by the press and interviewed. Whereas each client has been paying one prostitute to play the same game with him, to collude with him – a sinner for the Bishop, a thief for the Judge, a horse for the General – when all the people respond to this man as a Bishop, this man as a Judge, that man as a General, the false Bishop becomes a real Bishop, the false Judge becomes a real Judge, the false General a true General, and Madame becomes Queen, in as true a sense as any person ever is a Bishop, General, Judge, or Queen.

The hero of the play, if there is one, is the Chief of Police. The Chief of Police has never yet been impersonated, but he feels he will know by a certain weakness in his muscles that the moment has come when he can cease to act, sit back, and restfully await death. He is presented as the only man who really acts in the course of the play. The others, if they were logical, would have to admit that even if they were what they were, Bishop, Judge, General, they would still be phoneys. The Chief of Police challenges them:

CHIEF OF POLICE: You've never performed an act for its own sake, but always so that, when linked with other acts, it would make a Bishop, a Judge, a General. . . .

THE BISHOP: That's both true and false. For each act contained within itself its leaven of novelty.

CHIEF OF POLICE: Forgive me, Monsignor, but this leaven of novelty was immediately nullified by the fact that the act turned on itself.

THE JUDGE: We acquired greater dignity thereby (p. 97).

The Chief of Police is not denied his happy ending. He has the satisfaction of being able to witness before the play ends, through a viewing-box, the leader of the Revolution, Roger, come to the brothel and be the first man who had ever wanted to play Chief of Police. To do this he must enter a Mausoleum which the entire people have slaved to build, where are tombs enshrined in tombs, cenotaphs in cenotaphs, coffins in coffins, all deathly silent, in which there is only the coldness of death, and the groaning of men who have slaved to hollow out this stone, in which it is proved that he is loved and that he is the victor.

Genet leaves it an open question whether or not, or in what sense, there can ever be anything other than collusive make-believe. Perhaps it is possible 'to see things as they are, to gaze at the world tranquilly and accept responsibility for the gaze, whatever it might see'. But the last word is with Madame.

IRMA: In a little while, I'll have to start all over again . . . put all the lights on again . . . dress up . . . [*a cock crows*] Dress up . . .

ah, the disguises! Distribute roles again ... assume my own ... [*she stops in the middle of the stage, facing the audience*]. Prepare yours ... judges, generals, bishops, chamberlains, rebels who allow the revolt to congeal. I'm going to prepare my costumes and studios for tomorrow. ... You must now go home, where everything – you can be quite sure – will be even falser than here. ... You must go now. You'll leave by the right, through the alley ... [*she extinguishes the last light*]. It's morning already [*a burst of machine-gun fire*].

The issues that Sartre and Genet have depicted in these plays implicate us all in every moment of our lives. The following are some examples from an analytic group of the search to find in 'the other' the 'complement' required to sustain collusive identity.[2]

The group consisted of seven men, aged from twenty-five to thirty-five. With one exception, they were quite successful middle-class people. Jack owned a garage, Bill worked in his father's grocery business. The exception was Richard, who had failed innumerable examinations and was now living at home with his mother, trying to recoup his energies for a further effort to become a chartered accountant.

In the early sessions the group assumed that it had come together to be dependent on the analyst. He should tell them what to do, ask questions, give advice. When he confined himself to being silent or making remarks about the situation, they decided, at the suggestion of Jack, who was apparently the most independent, that he must be waiting in order to help them and that their best way to help him to help them was to talk about themselves. He took the role of leader, asked questions, drew people out, directed the discussion along the lines of difficulties with women, smoothed over tensions, and spoke a bit about his own feelings, mainly about

2. The data upon which this account is based are drawn from complete sound-recordings of group meetings.

women. The group warmed to this, with the exception of Bill. He spoke to the others on his own initiative, but not often, and never spontaneously to Jack. When occasionally asked a question by Jack, he answered laconically. Jack seemed slightly put out that Bill did not respond to his lead like the others.

In the fifth session, there developed the usual discussion about women, led by Jack, in which everyone participated except Bill. The latter, apparently quite irrelevantly, broke in on this discussion to express vehemently his dislike of football, and the crowds who went to see football. It was an unintelligent game and football fans were stupid people with whom he could feel nothing in common. All the others went to football matches. Jack also: not however, he said, for the football but because he wanted to be 'one of the boys'. Bill went on about how much he longed to meet someone with common interests, who shared his appreciation of the arts, who was not just the same as all the other dull uninteresting people, beginning with his father, who could not see his true value. Jack took him up by commenting that artists enjoy discussing art with each other. Bill said: 'Yes, I'm a bit of an artist, I like to dabble.' Jack then remarked that football fans also enjoyed talking football, but Bill ignored this and went on to speak of the appreciation of painting. Jack said, however, that only very well-educated people could really appreciate art. This was a distinctly unencouraging comment to make to Bill, who was very sensitive about his lack of formal education. However, a precarious *rapprochement* was established when at Jack's suggestion it was agreed that anyone could appreciate music.

Bill wished to see himself and to be seen as a superior person with superior tastes, but he never could discount entirely the feeling that he counted for nothing with those who really mattered. He felt he could never 'really' become anybody because, despite anything he himself might do, he was made of the same flesh and blood as his parents, and they were 'empty, dull and uninteresting'. He saw me, however, with all the attributes of the ideal 'other'. As an analyst, I was strong, educated, understanding, and appreciative. Unfortunately, however, I was also able to distinguish true from fake. In despair of being a genuine person himself, he felt empty; therefore in need of 'getting' something from me. He often expressed disappointment that 'in this technique' the analyst did not give him more. The analyst, the 'ideal other', was also frustrating and unsatisfying. His 'technique' was 'unexciting', 'dull, empty, and uninteresting'. In his despair at being himself, the more he felt empty, the more the analyst was a dense being, who embodied all he lacked. The analyst's penis became the emblem of all the analyst's attributes, which he longed to incorporate. This found expression in passive homosexual longings towards me as the ideal other, which he revealed in a letter. The others in the group avoided passive homosexual orientation by carefully seeing themselves as men, for whom the relevant other was always a women. Their evocation of the presence of women, in their absence, was a 'defence' against homosexual intra-group tensions.

Like Bill, Jack felt his parents had given him nothing, or not enough, or the wrong sort of things. He, however, was full of aspirations to be a good husband and parent himself, and a good patient. He wanted to *give* all the time, and displayed his need to do this by the role he assumed. However, to his dismay, he always resented those he 'loved', namely those to whom he felt impelled to give. He defined his 'neurosis' as the inability to stop resenting those he loved for what he gave them.

These two, Bill and Jack, began to form a collusive relationship based on each confirming the other in a false position. Bill was confirmed by Jack in his illusionary superiority and in his false premise of his essential worthlessness. Bill confirmed Jack's illusion of being a 'giver'. The collusive confirmation of each false self is the obverse of genuine confirmation. Their closeness counterfeited genuine friendship. Jack, in his own eyes, was an independent, hard-headed, matter-of-fact, down-to-earth businessman, extremely heterosexual, although women for him were only those absent presences he talked about with 'the boys'. He was in no one's debt and very generous.

Bill dreamt of far-away places where things could be beautiful and people were refined, not vulgar and coarse like here and now. People knew nothing of finer things. What, one might imagine, could Jack give that he wanted, or vice versa?

One thing was clear in listening to them. When they talked together Jack was never more 'Jack' as Jack saw himself, and Bill was never more 'Bill' as he saw himself. Each confirmed the other in his illusionary identity. Each concealed from the other what could break this up. This was so until Bill began to imply that he had sexual feelings towards Jack. This Jack could not take.

The group behaved 'as if' the pairing were sexual, and thereby denied that it was *really*, along with the other aspects of the collusion they chose not to notice. Jack asked Bill what he thought about when he masturbated. Bill said, after some coaxing, that he sometimes thought about a man. Jack quickly said that he always thought of women, and immediately checked with the others that they did the same. This was his way of writing off Bill. This was one point at which the collusion seemed to end; although rejection was itself part of the collusion. The sexual other for Jack had to be feminine and he could not stand being the sexual other to a man.

The other group members each reacted in his own way to

this uneasy collusion. The clearest expression of anxiety came from a man who had always thought his parents damaged each other, and feared hurting his wife. He was particularly sensitive to Jack's aggression towards and rejection of Bill. During one of their somewhat sado-masochistic exchanges, Jack attacked Bill for not going to football matches. This man broke in to say he was feeling faint, as he had done the night before at the sight of a boxing match on television when one boxer gave the other a horrible beating.

Richard was the only one who seemed to wish the collusion to go on indefinitely. He was an extremely schizoid individual. Once, recently, he had left his books to have a walk in the park. It was a beautiful evening in early autumn. As he sat watching the lovers together, and the sun setting, he began to feel at one with the whole scene, with the whole of nature, with the cosmos. He got up and ran home in a panic. With relief he 'came to himself' again. Richard's identity could be sustained only in isolation. Relationship threatened loss of identity – being engulfed, fused, merged, losing separate distinctiveness. He could only *be* by himself, but the sight of people together fascinated him. It seemed so impossible for him, so remote from what was within his reach, that he was barely jealous or envious. His inner self was empty. He longed to be together with anyone. But he could not be separate if he was attached. If he were attached to anyone he would be a clam, a leech as he expressed it. He was 'outside' life. He could only be a spectator. When Jack asked him an 'objectively' harmless question his reply was that he felt his existence threatened by questions, and immediately asked Bill what he thought. He could only be a *voyeur*. This suggests that such collusive pairing was something that Richard was not *able* to do. Playing the same game is at least doing something together with another. It implies some measure of freedom from those worst fears of destroying or being destroyed by the other, which can virtually preclude the possibility of any relation with anyone on any terms.[3]

It is in terms of basic frustration of the self's search for a collusive complement for false identity that Freud's dictum that analysis should be conducted under conditions of maximal frustration takes on its most cogent meaning.

It is worth examining the 'place' of the therapist in such a group, and the 'place' the persons in the group feel themselves to have in relation to him.

One basic function of genuinely analytical or existential therapy is the provision of a setting in which as little as possible impedes each person's capacity to discover his own self.

Without beginning to enter into a full discussion of this, one can comment on one aspect of the therapist's position. The therapist's intention is not to allow himself to collude with the patients in adopting a position in their phantasy-system: and, alternatively, not to use the patients to embody any phantasy of his own.

The group was frequently dominated by a phantasy, expressed in the issue of whether I had the answer to their problems. Their problem was to decide if I had or had not 'the answer'; and if I had, how to extract it from me. My function was not to collude in either the group's illusionment or its disillusionment, and to try to articulate the underlying phantasy-systems.

A large part of the art of therapy is in the tact and lucidity with which the analyst points out the ways in which collusion maintains illusions or disguises delusions. The dominant phantasy in a group may be that the therapist has 'the answer', and that if they had 'the answer' they would not suffer. The therapist's task is then like the Zen Master's, to point out that

3. The foregoing account is a modified version of an earlier publication (Laing and Esterson, 1958).

suffering is not due to not getting 'the answer', but *is* the very state of desire that assumes the existence of that kind of answer, and the frustration of never getting it. As Burtt (1955) says of the teachings of Hsi Yun, the Zen Master of about A.D. 840, his intention was to make the questioner aware 'that the real difficulty is not so much in his questions being unanswerable as in his continuing in the state of mind that leads him to ask them' (p. 195). Illusionment or disillusionment may equally be based on the same phantasy. There is 'an answer' somewhere; or there is 'no answer' anywhere. The same issue either way.

Therapy without collusion cannot help but frustrate desires generated by phantasy.

CHAPTER 9

False and Untenable Positions

1. INDUCED BY SELF

*Nam in omni actione principaliter intenditur ab
agente, sive necessitate naturae sive voluntarie agat,
propriam similitudinem explicare; unde fit quod
omne agens, inquantum huiusmodi, delectatur, quia,
cum omne quod est appetat suum esse, ac in agendo
agentis esse quodammodo amplietur, sequitur de
necessitare delectatio.... Nihil igitur agit nisi tale
existens quale patiens fieri debet.*

DANTE[1]

ONE speaks of being put in a false position, or in an untenable
position. Persons put themselves and others, and are in turn
put by others, into false or untenable positions. In developing
a theory of alienation in this sense, one will be wise to give
ear to two sets of colloquialisms which point to the *position*
one can put oneself or the other into, and to the position one
may be put in by others. It is everyday common-sense knowledge that a person can put himself into a false or untenable
position and be put in a false or untenable position by others.
Position is here used in an existential sense rather than as

1. 'For in every action what is primarily intended by the doer, whether
he acts from natural necessity or out of free will, is the disclosure of his
own image. Hence it comes about that every doer, in so far as he does,
takes delight in doing; since everything that is desires its own being, and
since in action the being of the doer is somehow intensified, delight
necessarily follows. ... Thus, nothing acts unless by acting it makes
patent its latent self.' As quoted and translated by Arendt (1958, p. 175).

economic or social-class position, or position in some other hierarchical system.

Everyday speech abounds in expressions about self's contribution to one's own experience of 'place' or 'position' in the world. One says that a person 'puts himself into' his acts, or that he is *not* 'in' what he says or does; a person's actions are commonly seen as ways he has of losing himself, or forgetting himself, of getting out of himself. He may seem to be 'full of himself' or 'beside himself', or to have 'come to himself' again after 'not being himself'. These expressions are attributions about the person's relation to his own actions, and are used quite 'naturally' as the language of 'the man in the street'. In them all the issue is the extent to which the act is seen or felt to *potentiate* the being or existence of the doer, or the extent to which the action, as Dante puts it in the above quotation, makes patent the latent self of the doer (even if the primary intention of the doer is not to disclose himself). An issue essential to an existential analysis of action is to what extent and in what ways the agent is disclosed or concealed, wittingly or unwittingly, intentionally or unintentionally, in and through action.

Everyday speech gives us clues we would be wise to follow. It hints that there may be a general law or principle that a person will feel himself to be going forward when he puts himself into his actions, presuming this to be equivalent to self-disclosure (making patent his true self), but that if this is not so, he will be liable to feel that he is 'going back' or is stationary, or 'going round in circles', or 'getting nowhere'. In 'putting myself into' what I do, I lose myself, and in so doing I seem to become myself. The act I do is felt to be me, and I become 'me' in and through such action. Also, there is a sense in which a person 'keeps himself alive' by his acts; each act can be a new beginning, a new birth, a re-creation of oneself, a self-fulfilling.

To be 'authentic' is to be true to oneself, to be what one is, to be 'genuine'. To be 'inauthentic' is to not be oneself, to be false to oneself: to be not as one appears to be, to be counterfeit. We tend to link the categories of truth and reality by saying that a genuine act is real, but that a person who habitually uses action as a masquerade is not real.

In everyday speech, and in more systematic theory which, to adapt a remark of William James, is but an unduly obstinate attempt to think clearly, 'authentic' action or 'inauthentic' action can be viewed from many angles: from each angle different features come to the fore.

The intensification of the being of the agent through self-disclosure, through making patent the latent self, is the meaning of Nietzsche's 'will to power'. It is the 'weak' man who, in lieu of potentiating himself genuinely, counterfeits his impotence by dominating and controlling others, by idealizing physical strength or sexual potency, in the restricted sense of the capacity to have erections and to ejaculate.

The act that is genuine, revealing, and potentiating is felt by me as fulfilling. This is the only *actual* fulfilment of which I can properly speak. It is an act that is me: in this action I am myself. I put myself 'in' it. In so far as I put myself 'into' what I do, I become myself through this doing. I know also that the converse is true, when I feel 'empty', or am haunted by futility. In the light of such impressions of myself, I am compelled to see the other. I suspect 'frantic' activity in another. I sense that *he* senses in his actions a lack of intrinsic meaning: that in clinging to external formulas and dogmas he senses his emptiness. I expect that such a person will envy and resent others. If, from my impression of myself, I see him as not fulfilling himself by not putting himself into his own future, I am alert to various ways in which he will try to fill his emptiness. One fills oneself with others (introjective identification) or lives vicariously by living through the lives of others (projective identification). One's 'own' life comes to a stop. One goes round in a circle, in a whirl, going everywhere and getting nowhere.

An existential phenomenology of action is concerned with the movements, the twists and turns, of the person as one who puts himself, in different ways, more or less, into what he does. It is concerned to elucidate on what one bases such judgements or attributions, whether about self or other. The psychiatrist may base a diagnosis of schizophrenia as much on what he considers the patient's relation to his actions to be, as on the acts themselves viewed as 'behaviour' pure and simple. If the psychiatrist or psychopathologist under the illusion that he sees the other person in a purely 'objective' way, fails to subject his diagnosis by 'signs' and 'symptoms' to a critical examination, he is condemned by these 'clinical' categories to an impoverished and twisted view of the other. Such 'clinical' categories as schizoid, autistic, 'impoverished' affect, 'withdrawal', all presuppose that there are reliable, valid impersonal criteria for making attributions about the other person's relation to his actions. There are no such reliable or valid criteria.

It is no simple oversight that such is the case, and the situation is unlikely to be remedied by someone setting up 'reliability' studies. The estrangement of *our own theory* from *our own actions* goes deep into our historical situation.

In our daily discourse, we employ, among others, two notions of 'truth'. One is the 'truth value' of a proposition; the relation of words to things. If A says 'p is the case', what is usually termed the 'truth value' of the proposition 'p is the case' has nothing to do with A's relationship to this proposition. However, in daily discourse, it is frequently more important for us to gauge A's relation to the proposition: whether A is telling the truth, whether he is lying, or whether he is deceiving himself, and so on.

Heidegger (1949) has contrasted the natural-scientific concept of truth with a notion of truth he finds in some of the
pre-Socratics. Whereas in natural science truth consists in a
correspondence, an *adaequatio*, between what goes on *in intellectu*
and what goes on *in re*, between the structure of a symbol
system 'in the mind' and the structure of events 'in the world',
another concept of truth is found in the Greek word ἀλήθεια.
In this concept, truth is literally that which is without secrecy,
what discloses itself without a veil. This concept has practical
interpersonal implications in terms of telling the truth, lying,
pretending, equivocating, by speech or deed: one constantly
seeks to gauge the person's 'position' in relation to his own
speech and deeds.

When one sees actions of the other in the light of this latter
form of truth or falsehood, one says a man is truthful or 'true
to himself' if one 'feels' he means what he says or says what
he means. His words, or his other ways of expressing himself,
are 'true' expressions of his 'real' experience or intentions.
Between such 'truth' and a lie there is room for the most
curious and subtle ambiguities and complexities in the person's disclosure or concealment of himself. One says with
confidence, 'His smile gave him away', or, 'That expression
is just put on', or, 'That rings true'. But what is revealed,
what concealed, to and from whom in the Giaconda smile, in
the 'twixt earnest and joke' of Blake's angel, in the infinite
pathos, or apathy, of a Harlequin of Picasso? The liar deceives
others without deceiving himself. The hysteric's deception of
himself is anterior to his deception of others. The actor's
actions are not 'him'. The hypocrite, the imposter – like
Mann's Felix Krull, absorbed in the parts he plays – are the
exploiters and victims of the fissure between self and expression. There is no final assurance that one can attribute correctly the other's relation to his actions. 'We look', writes
Hegel (1949, p. 345),

at a man's face and see whether he is in earnest with what he says or does. Conversely, however, what is here intended to be an expression of the inner is at the same time an existent objective expression, and hence itself falls to the level of mere existence which is absolutely contingent for the self-conscious individual. It is therefore no doubt an expression, but at the same time only in the sense of a sign, so that to the content expressed the peculiar nature of that by which it is expressed is completely indifferent. The inner, in thus appearing, is doubtless an invisible made visible, but without being itself united to this appearance. It can just as well make use of some other appearance as another inner can adopt the same appearance. Lichtenberg, therefore, is right in saying: 'Suppose the physiognomist ever did have a man in his grasp, it would merely require a courageous resolution on the man's part to make himself again incomprehensible for centuries.'

'I am going to the House of my Lord', the Christian slave would say, challenged by the Roman soldier. Such equivocation plays upon the inexorable separateness *between* man and man, that no love, nor the most complete experience of union, completely or permanently annuls.

When a man's words, gestures, acts, disclose his real intentions, one says they are genuine and not counterfeit as coin is genuine and not counterfeit. His frown of disapproval, his word of encouragement, his smile of pleasure, are the true and genuine currency of himself.

Actions may be attributed, by self to self or self to other, as revealing or concealing, 'strong' or 'weak', 'fulfilling' or 'emptying'; making 'real' the being of the doer, making him more 'unreal', more creative, or more destructive.

The man who does not reveal himself or is not 'seen' by the others when he does, may turn, in partial despair, to other modes of self-disclosure. The exhibitionist shows off his body, or a part of his body, or some highly prized function or skill trying to overcome that haunting isolation and loneliness of one who feels his 'real' or 'true' self has never been disclosed to and confirmed by others. The man who compulsively exhibits his penis substitutes disclosure through this 'thing' rather than through living. Analysis of such a person can show that it is not just this thing that he would have others gasp at, but himself, whose actions are 'weak', 'phoney', 'unreal', and impress no one. He wishes to put his would-be 'true' self into his penis. But instead of making patent his latent self and thereby 'intensifying' his being, he holds himself in (inhibits himself) and holds out (exhibits) his penis.

The person in a false position may not be aware of being 'in' such a position. Only to the extent that he is not completely 'in' this position, that he is not totally estranged from his 'own' experience and actions, can he experience his position *as false*. Perhaps without his realizing it his 'life' comes to a stop. With no real future of his own, he may be in that supreme despair which is, as Kierkegaard says, not to know he is in despair. He is in despair because he has lost 'his own' future, and so can have no genuine hope or trust in any future. The person in a false position has lost a starting-point of his own from which to throw or thrust himself, that is, to project himself, forward. He has lost the place. He does not know where he is or where he is going. He cannot get anywhere however hard he tries. In despair, just as one place is the same as another, so one time is the same as another. The future is the resultant of the present, the present is the resultant of the past, and past is unalterable.

Such realizations may break through in dreams. We stated above that no matter how hectically a person may move about in space or engage in business or affairs, if all this is 'false', 'he', existentially considered, is not getting anywhere. He remains 'in a whirl', 'going round in circles'. No matter how hard he runs he is never moving from the same spot. Such a man has the following dream:

I was at the seashore. There were sands and barren rocks. I was alone. I ran into the sea and swam and swam until, almost exhausted, I came to another shore, where there were again sands and barren rocks. Once more I was alone. I found that it was the same place.

The person who dreamt this was apparently successful. Existentially, swimming only got him to the same place.

A common paranoid delusion is that there is a plot directed against the self. Self attributes to others the intention to oust self from his position in the world, to displace and replace him. How this is to be effected is often left vague and 'unsystematized'.

Dostoyevsky, in his early story *The Double*, makes Golyadkin write in a letter to a colleague (1958, pp. 164-5):

In conclusion, I beg that you will convey to these persons that their strange pretensions, and their ignoble and chimerical desire *to oust others from the places that they occupy by their very existence in the world, and to supplant them* [italics mine], are deserving of consternation, contempt and pity, and what is more, qualify them for the madhouse. Moreover, attitudes such as these are strictly forbidden by law, and in my opinion quite justly so. There are limits to everything, and if this is a joke, it is a pretty poor one. I will say more – it is utterly immoral for I venture to assure you, Sir, that my own ideas about keeping *one's place*, and these I have amplified above, are purely moral.

I have the honour to remain, Sir,

Y. GOLYADKIN.

Dostoyevsky not only describes the phenomenology of Golyadkin's displacement from the 'position' he occupies by his very existence in the world, and of his eventual replacement by the double: he shows how this 'delusion' is intimately connected with Golyadkin's own secret intention *not to be himself*. It is his own intention that he attributes to the others. He

himself is ousting himself from the place in the world his very
existence entitles him to.

Shortly before he meets his double for the first time, 'on a
wet and windy St Petersburg night', Dostoyevsky states:

... Any detached and impartial observer who at that moment
merely glanced at Mr Golyadkin and saw his anguished step, would
immediately have been imbued with a sense of the appalling horror
of his misfortunes, and would certainly have said he had the look
of a man wishing to hide and escape from himself. And that is
exactly how it was. We will say more: *at that moment Mr Golyadkin
wanted not only to escape from himself, but to annihilate himself completely,
to return to dust and cease to be* (p. 73, italics my own).

After his encounter with his double, he discovers that this
man is ousting him in every possible way from his position in
existence until he completely takes his place in the world.
Yet just before he is taken away to the madhouse, Golyadkin
has a glimpse of his 'pernicious twin', whom he sees for a
moment as 'apparently not pernicious at all, not even his
twin, but a stranger and a perfectly amiable person in his own
right' (p. 246).

While he had come to feel that this other was ousting him
completely from his place in the world, while he was dreaming
that the whole of St Petersburg was peopled by other Golyad-
kins, he himself had been intentionally seeking to annihilate
himself, seeking not to be himself. This project at the very
heart of his existence was a secret even from himself that he
remained unable to grasp, unable to realize. He would at other
times experience himself as 'a man losing control of himself,
losing sight of himself, on the point of vanishing for ever ... '
(p. 220). Yet even at this point, when he is about to cease to
exist and he is ruined, he again intentionally tries a further
method of not being himself in a last effort to remedy the
situation.

'That's the best thing,' he thought, 'I'd better try a different approach. This is what I'll do – I'll just be an outside observer, and nothing more. I'm an onlooker, an outsider, that's all, I'll say. And whatever happens it won't be me who's to blame. That's it. That's how it will be now.'

And our hero did indeed do as he had decided and went back, and went back the more readily for having, thanks to a happy thought, become an outsider.

'It's the best thing. You're not answerable for anything, and you'll see what you should' (p. 242).

In practice, one can never jump to conclusions. Lemert (1967) describes almost the only series of paranoid delusions where the real actual others were investigated. Lemert's view is that much more often than is generally supposed there is some sort of conspiracy around people who feel conspired against. The reverberating cross-attributions in such circumstances are very complex indeed, and it is strange that there has been so little attempt to follow up Lemert's work (see Scheff, 1967, and Laing and Esterson, 1964).

2. INDUCED BY OTHERS

Where you are there arises a place.

RILKE

Children should be seen and not heard.

One can put oneself into a false position, ultimately into an untenable position. One *can be put* into a false position also, ultimately into an untenable position, by the actions of others.

Colloquial speech again supplies us with many expressions. To put someone on the spot; to give someone room to move; to have no elbow-room; to be put in an awkward position; to make someone feel small; to know where one is with someone; to pull someone or to be pulled in opposite directions; to turn the screw on; to know where one stands; to have the ground taken from under one's feet; to be boxed in, tied in a knot, caught, sat upon, cornered, entangled, trapped, smothered.

To understand fully the one person's experience of his 'position' obviously one requires to know the actions of the others, as well as his own actions and his own imaginary and phantasy others.

The amount of 'room' to move a person feels that he has is related both to *the room that he gives himself and the room he is given by others.*

This is dramatically illustrated by the report of a policeman who watched a little boy running round a block of flats. After the boy had run past him on his way round the block for the twentieth time, the policeman finally asked him what he was doing. The boy said he was running away from home, but his father wouldn't let him cross the road! The boy's 'free space' was curtailed by his 'internalization' of this paternal injunction.

The space, geometrical and metaphorical, of both adult and child, is highly structured by the influence of others, one way or the other, all the time. This is 'common sense', a truism, but it becomes necessary to state this when a phenomenology of space neglects to give due weight to this factor.[2] In considering some aspects of the contribution others make to the person's existential position, we shall find that a number of the considerations raised earlier come together in the understanding of 'false' position and 'untenable' position.

To understand the 'position' from which a person lives, it is necessary to know the original sense of his place in the world he grew up with. His own sense of his place will have been developed partly in terms of what place he will have been *given* in the first instance by the nexus of original others.

2. In particular I refer to the pioneering studies of Minkowski (1933, 1953). The same criticism is applicable to Binswanger (1958).

Every human being, whether child or adult, seems to require *significance*, that is, *place in another person's world*. Adults and children seek 'position' in the eyes of others, a position that offers room to move. It is difficult to imagine many who would choose unlimited freedom within a nexus of personal relations, if anything they did had no significance for anyone else. Would anyone choose freedom if nothing he did mattered to anyone? It seems to be a universal human desire to wish to occupy a place in the world of at least one other person. Perhaps the greatest solace in religion is the sense that one lives in the Presence of an Other. Most people at some time in their lives seek the experience, whether or not they have found it in early life, of occupying *first* place, if not the only significant place, in at least one other person's world. As argued earlier, no comprehensive theory of man–woman relations can neglect the frequent observation that each seeks not only another to love, and be loved by, but another that self feels is gratified by being loved by self. Imagine an ideal love affair without the last ingredient. Jill loves Jack. Jack loves Jill. Jill knows that Jack loves Jill. Jack knows that Jill loves Jack. But Jack says it does not make any difference to him whether Jill loves him or not. As long as he loves her that is all that matters. How will Jill feel?

In typical paranoid ideas of reference, the person feels that the murmurings and mutterings he hears as he walks past a street crowd are about him. In a bar, a burst of laughter behind his back is at some joke cracked about him. When one gets to know such a person more than superficially, one often discovers that what tortures him is not so much his delusions of reference, but his harrowing suspicion that he is of no importance to anyone, that no one is referring to him at all.

What constantly preoccupies and torments the paranoid is usually the precise opposite of what at first is most apparent. He is persecuted by being the centre of everyone else's world, yet he is preoccupied with the thought that he never occupies first place in anyone's affection. He is often prone to obsessive jealousy – that cold jealousy Minkowski (1933) has described in the paranoid – a jealousy without love, occurring within a profoundly different 'lived' space from the usual. Unable to experience himself as significant for another, he develops a delusionally significant place for himself *in the world of others*. Others see him as living in a world of his own. Ironically this is true and not true. For there is also a sense that he lives not so much in his own world, but in the empty place he supposes he does *not* occupy in the *others'* world. He appears to be profoundly self-centred, but the more self-centred he appears, the more he is trying to convince himself that he is the centre of *their* world.

Peter (Laing, 1960) was a young man who was preoccupied with guilt *because* he occupied a place in the world, even in a physical sense. He could not realize, make real to himself, that he had the right to have any presence for others. Unable to realize his actual presence, he filled in this gap in his realization of himself by phantasy experience that tended to become more and more delusional.

A peculiar aspect of his childhood was that his presence in the world was largely ignored. No weight was given to the fact that he was in the same room while his parents had intercourse. He had been physically cared for in that he had been well fed and kept warm, and underwent no physical separation from his parents during his earlier years. Yet he had been consistently treated as though he did not 'really' exist. Perhaps worse than the experience of physical separation was to be in the same room as his parents and ignored, not malevolently, but through sheer indifference. For as long as he could remember, he had felt uneasily guilty simply at having presence for others, or at wanting to be present for others. Instead of real-izing a sense of his own presence for others, he developed a delusional sense of his presence for others. He believed that to make his presence felt he would have to go to such extremes that no one would want to have anything to do with him, and thus he came to make the central enterprise of his life to be nobody.

This man's primal-scene memories and his consequent phantasy prototype of triadic situations were characterized not so much by jealousy and anger on his part, and subsequent guilt and anxiety, as by *shame and despair* that he did not seem able to make any difference to his parents in any way. He felt himself to be only an additional part of the furniture of their lives which they cared for as they cared for their other material possessions.

Peter, *p*, had no place in the world in his own eyes, and he did not believe that he occupied a place in *o*'s world either. The situation was schematically as follows: *p*'s view of *o*'s view of him is that *o* does not see him. On the basis of these gaps in the existential fabric of his, *p*'s, identity, he constructs a delusional presence for *o*. He complains that he stinks in *other* people's nostrils.

The paranoid person typically complains of the view of *p* that *p* attributes to *o*, $p \rightarrow (o \rightarrow p)$.

The person experiences, not the absence of the presence of the other, but the absence of his own presence as other for the other. He is haunted by the other who does not act towards him in any way whatever, who does not wish to seduce him, rape him, steal anything from him, smother him, eat him up, or in any way destroy him. The other is there, but *he* is not there to the other. It is not correct to say that he is projecting his *own* greed on to the other. It is rather common for such people to feel *very* greedy, and to feel very greedy *and* envious. This is on all secondary, tertiary, quaternary, turns of a spiral that does not *start* from constitutional envy. Everyone to begin with is constitutionally alive. I have never ever come across anyone who is alive as most babies still are, at least for a few weeks after birth, envy life in any other creature. The baby who is alive delights in life. Constitutionally, life dances with life.

We shall now consider some ways in which the others in speech and deed do destroy life.

There have been a number of studies in this field in the last decade. Here I shall consider three of these studies.

An article by Searles (1959), 'The Effort to Drive the Other Person Crazy', one of the early contributions to this subject, lists six modes of driving the other person crazy, 'each of these techniques tends to undermine the other person's confidence in his own emotional reactions and his own perception of reality'. They can be formulated as follows:

1. *p* repeatedly calls attention to areas of the personality of which *o* is dimly aware, areas quite at variance with the kind of person *o* considers himself or herself to be.

2. *p* stimulates *o* sexually in a situation in which it would be disastrous for *o* to seek gratification.

3. *p* simultaneously exposes *o* to stimulation and frustration or to rapidly alternating stimulation and frustration.

4. *p* relates to *o* at simultaneously unrelated levels (e.g. sexually and intellectually).

5. *p* switches from one emotional wavelength to another while on the same topic (being 'serious' and then being 'funny' about the same thing).

6. *p* switches from one topic to the next while maintaining the same emotional wavelength (e.g. a matter of life and death is discussed in the same manner as the most trivial happening).

In Searles's view 'the striving' to drive the other person crazy is predominantly at an unconscious level, but one ingredient in a complex of pathogenic relatedness beyond the capacity of either participant to control fully.

In general, '. . . the initiating of any kind of interpersonal interaction that tends to activate various areas of his personality in opposition to one another – tends to drive him crazy (i.e. schizophrenic)'. It seems to me that this formulation does not do justice to the data Searles brings forward. To say that the initiation of any kind of interpersonal interaction that tends to foster emotional conflict in the other person tends to drive him crazy, is not sufficiently specific. There are many ways for one person to confront another with two or more conflicting courses of action. To imply that to promote conflict is, in itself, liable to disintegrate the person put into conflict, seems to confuse conflict that may sharpen a person's being with what may sabotage and destroy self, unless self has exceptional means of coping.

The techniques used by Laura to undermine the Captain's self-confidence in Strindberg's *The Father* are convincing. But they are effective only with someone who has little resistance to them. This opens up the study of techniques of coping with or resisting schizogenic situations. Techniques of brain-washing, which Searles likens to schizogenic activity, and techniques of resisting being brainwashed are only partially relevant. Brainwashers are trying to undermine their victims' ideology and to replace it with another, they are not trying to drive their victims crazy. If they do, they have failed in their objective, to replace one structure by another.

What is more specific is interpersonal action which tends to *confuse* or *mystify* (Laing, 1965). This makes it difficult for the one person to know 'who' he is, 'who' the other is, and what is the situation they are 'in'. He does not know 'where he is' any more.

The examples Searles gives of various modes of driving the other person crazy are all of this order. For instance, a man who persistently questions 'the adjustment' of his wife's younger sister so that she becomes increasingly anxious. In questioning his sister-in-law he repeatedly calls attention to areas of her personality which are at variance with the person she considers herself to be. Since psychotherapists also do this, the question arises when such a manoeuvre is liberating and when not.

This is a very important type of interpersonal disjunction. Sister-in-law's system of self-attributions, her self-picture ($p \to p$) is disjunctive with other's view of her as implied in the man's questions. Such interpersonal disjunction does not necessarily *force* a person to split himself, unless that person feels obliged to comply with the other's view of him, to take up the position ascribed to him explicitly or implicitly by the other. If a person already does not know 'where he is', to question 'adjustment', to attribute falsity to 'adjusted' actions, is extremely confusing. In other circumstances it could be clarifying. One could become very confused if the other both 'accused' one of not being adjusted, and at the same time 'cast doubts' on the validity of 'adjusted' actions, as though to accuse one simultaneously of not being adjusted and of being adjusted.

To stimulate the other sexually in a context in which it is forbidden to gratify aroused sexual desire again involves not only conflict but confusion, namely, *doubt about how the 'situation' itself has to be defined*.

Searles notes that in innumerable instances 'we have records of the parent of a schizophrenic patient who behaved in an inordinately seductive way towards the child, thus fostering in the latter an intense conflict between sexual needs on the one hand, and regular super-ego retaliations . . . on the other. This circumstance,' he says, 'can be seen as productive of a conflict in the child between, on the one hand, his desire to mature and fulfil his own individuality, and, on the other hand, his regressive desire to remain in an infantile symbiosis with his parent, to remain there at the cost of investing even his sexual strivings, which constitute his trump card in the game of self-realization, in that regressive relationship.'

This again appears to be a special kind of disjunction, in which the person cannot see clearly the 'real' issues that face him. For the child, the issue may be: Do I love my mother or father or not? What must I do to keep him or her alive? Am I selfish if I do not respond to their way of loving me? Am I ungrateful if I do not comply with what they wish of me? The 'real' issues may be *unrealized*. The basic real choice before him may be: 'to be himself' at the expense of losing his symbiotic relationship with the parent; or, to maintain a symbiosis at the expense of losing autonomy. This issue is clear-cut. But one seldom finds a clear-cut realization of it. It is usually shrouded by the phantasy-system shared with the family. This phantasy-system, its content and its modality as phantasy, are often apparent to a perceptive outsider. The content of the phantasy is often known in part by the participants. What they seldom *realize* is that its modality is phantasy. Mother tells daughter, who in confiding some problem to her school-teacher has spoken to someone other than her mother about herself for the first time in her life, 'You'll see what a mess you'll get into, if you tell strangers these things. No one loves you like I do – no one understands you like I do.' Daughter came to believe that everyone in the world besides mother was a stranger, and every relationship with these strangers, including her father, was fraught with danger. Daughter could not afford to lose her relationship with mother because she believed, and felt, that no bond with anyone else was trustworthy. She shared with her mother the belief that any intention to break the bond with her mother was an expression of selfishness and ingratitude on her part for all that her mother had given her.

Therapy with such cases entails coming to look at the assumptions made on the basis of shared phantasy-systems. The disjunction must be *seen*. Once seen, and faced for the first time, confusion is converted to conflict. This involves emergence from a shared phantasy dread of separation. The act of leaving is felt as suicide or murder, or both. In disentangling the parent's phantasy from the patient's experience, the patient gets clear of this particular possibility of psychosis. True conflict is clarifying. False conflict is muddling. When the 'issue' is false and confused, the 'real' or 'true' conflict cannot come into focus, 'true' choices are not available, and the person is in danger of psychosis.

The simultaneous or rapidly alternating stimulus of other needs in addition to sexual ones, the exploitation of the child's desire to be helpful to the parent by making chronic pleas for sympathy, the technique of relation to the other on two different levels at the one time, are examples of confusion. Peter confuses Paul as to the person Paul is, and as to 'the situation' he is in.

In an *untenable position*, no matter how he feels or how he acts, or what meaning the situation has, his feelings are denuded of validity, his acts are stripped of their motives, intentions, and consequences, the situation is robbed of its meaning. This may be done unintentionally, as a by-product of each person's self-deception. Those who deceive themselves are obliged to deceive others. It is impossible for me to maintain a false picture of myself unless I falsify your picture of yourself and of me. I must disparage you if you are genuine, accuse you of being a phoney when you comply with what I want, say you are selfish if you go your own way, ridicule you for being immature if you try to be unselfish, and so on. The person caught within such a muddle does not know whether he is coming or going. In these circumstances what we call psychosis may be a desperate effort to hold on to something.

It is not surprising that the something may be what we call 'delusions'.

A group of workers at Palo Alto described a pattern well known now as the 'double-bind' situation. The 'victim' is caught in a tangle of paradoxical injunctions, or of attributions having the force of injunctions, in which he cannot do the right thing.

Their thesis is stated as follows (Bateson *et al.*, 1956):

The necessary ingredients for a double bind situation, as we see it are:

1. *Two or more persons.* Of these, we designate one, for purposes of our definition, as the 'victim'. We do not assume that the double bind is inflicted by the mother alone, but that it may be done either by mother alone or by some combination of mother, father, and/or siblings.

2. *Repeated experience.* We assume that the double bind is a recurrent theme in the experience of the victim. Our hypothesis does not invoke a single traumatic experience, but such repeated experience that the double bind structure comes to be an habitual expectation.

3. *A primary negative injunction.* This may have either of two forms: (*a*) 'Do not do so and so, I will punish you.' Here we select a context of learning based on avoidance of punishment rather than a context of reward seeking. There is perhaps no formal reason for this selection. We assume that the punishment may be either the withdrawal of love or the expression of hate or anger – or most devastating – the kind of abandonment that results from the parent's expression of extreme helplessness.[3]

4. *A secondary injunction conflicting with the first at a more abstract level, and like the first enforced by punishment or signals which threaten survival.* This secondary injunction is more difficult to describe than

3. The authors state in a footnote that their concept of punishment is being refined. It appears to involve perceptual experience in a way that cannot be encompassed by the notion of 'trauma'. See especially Jackson (1957) for the development of the concept of 'covert trauma'.

the primary for two reasons. First, the secondary injunction is commonly communicated to the child by non-verbal means. Posture, gesture, tone of voice, meaningful action, and the implications concealed in verbal comment may all be used to convey this more abstract message. Second, the secondary injunction may impinge upon any element of the primary prohibition. Verbalization of the secondary injunction may, therefore, include a wide variety of forms; for example, 'Do not see this as punishment'; 'Do not see me as the punishing agent'; 'Do not submit to my prohibitions'; 'Do not think of what you must not do'; 'Do not question my love of which the primary prohibition is (or is not) an example'; and so on. Other examples become possible when the double bind is inflicted not by one individual but by two. For example, one parent may negate at a more abstract level the injunctions of the other.

5. *A tertiary negative injunction prohibiting the victim from escaping from the field.* In a formal sense it is perhaps unnecessary to list this injunction as a separate item since the reinforcement at the other two levels involves a threat to survival, and if the double binds are imposed during infancy, escape is naturally impossible. However, it seems that in some cases the escape from the field is made impossible by certain devices which are not purely negative, e.g. capricious promises of love, and the like.

6. Finally, the complete set of ingredients is no longer necessary when the victim has learned to perceive his universe in double bind patterns. Almost any part of a double bind sequence may then be sufficient to precipitate panic or rage. The pattern of conflicting injunctions may even be taken over by hallucinatory voices.

The double bind involves two or more persons, of whom one is regarded as the 'victim'. Bateson and his associates propose that it will be difficult for a person to be sane who has been exposed to such a situation repeatedly, and put forward the hypothesis that 'there will be a breakdown in *any* individual's ability to discriminate between Logical Types whenever a double bind situation occurs' (italics my own).

One person conveys to the other that he should do something, and at the same time conveys on another level that he should not, or that he should do something else incompatible with it. The situation is sealed off for the 'victim' by a further injunction forbidding him or her to get out of the situation, or to dissolve it by commenting on it. The 'victim' is thus in an 'untenable' position. He cannot make a move without catastrophe. For example:

A mother visits her son, who has just been recovering from a mental breakdown.[4] As he goes towards her

(a) she opens her arms for him to embrace her, and/or

(b) to embrace him.

(c) As he gets nearer she freezes and stiffens.

(d) He stops irresolutely.

(e) She says, 'Don't you want to kiss your mummy?' – and as he still stands irresolutely

(f) she says, 'But dear, you mustn't be afraid of your feelings.'

He responds to her invitation to kiss her, but her posture, freezing, tension, simultaneously tell him not to. That she is frightened of a close relationship with him, or for some other reason does not want him actually to do what she invites him to do, cannot be openly admitted by the mother, and remains unsaid by her and the son. He responds to the 'unsaid', the unspoken message, 'Although I am holding my arms out for you to come and kiss me I am really frightened of you doing so, but can't admit this to myself or to you, so I hope you will be too "ill" to do so.' But then she indicates that she quite

4. This is a slightly modified and abridged version of an example given in the paper under notice. One should note that the analysis of the interaction is incomplete, since the description of the situation given does not include observations on the ways in which the patient may have been inducing the double-binding behaviour in the mother. For instance, between steps (b) and (c) above, the patient in moving towards his mother may have succeeded, by minute nuances in his expression and walk, in putting into his mother *his* fear of closeness with her, so that she stiffened.

simply wants him to kiss her, and implies that the reason why he does not kiss her is not because he has perceived her anxiety lest he do, or her command not to, but because he does not love her. When he does not answer, she implies that the reason why he has not kissed her is because he fears his sexual or aggressive feelings towards her. She conveys, in effect, 'Do not embrace me, or I will punish you,' *and* 'If you do not do so, I will punish you.' The 'punishment' will itself be secret.

This is an example of, on the surface, a simple incident. The suggestion is that a person persistently exposed from birth to situations of this kind will find it difficult to distinguish levels. The possible strategies for living out this untenable position that Bateson and his colleagues deduce from it, match the types of behaviour identified clinically as schizophrenia.

It is perhaps necessary to emphasize that we are not intending to give a balanced account of actual relationships, but are trying to illustrate possible types of disjunctive relations. *We are trying to describe how one person or a 'nexus' of persons can act towards another person.* How persons 'act towards' one another may have little to do with motives, or intentions, or with actual effects on the other. We are largely restricting ourselves to an exposition in dyadic terms, whereas in real life there probably will be at least three persons (*sic:* Weakland, 1960) involved. One step at a time.

One must remember that the child may put his parents into untenable positions. The baby cannot be satisfied. It cries 'for' the breast. It cries when the breast is presented. It cries when the breast is withdrawn. Unable to 'click with' or 'get through', mother becomes intensely anxious and feels hopeless. She withdraws from the baby in one sense, and becomes over-solicitous in another sense. Double binds can be two-way.

The double-bind hypothesis contains a number of sub-hypotheses, some of which seem more sound than others. A theory of 'modes of communication' is formulated in terms of Logical Types. It is doubtful if the Logical Type theory, which arises in the course of the construction of a calculus of propositions, can be applied directly to communication. Such 'modes of communication' certainly occur frequently in families of schizophrenics. To what extent double binds of what kind go on in other families is still not certain.

The work of the Palo Alto group, along with the Bethesda, Harvard, and other studies has, however, *revolutionized* the concept of what is meant by 'environment' and has already rendered obsolete most earlier discussions on the relevance of 'environment' to the origins of schizophrenia.

An interesting possibility is a link-up of this type of theory with recent biological theory.

A child runs away from danger. In flight from danger it runs to mother. At a certain stage, flight to mother and clinging to her may be a pre-potent behavioural pattern in reaction to danger. It is possible that 'flight' and 'clinging' to the mother are compounded of component instinctual response systems in the child that can be modified at certain stages only to a limited extent.

Let us suppose a situation wherein the mother herself is the object that generates danger, for whatever reason. If this happens when the pre-potent reaction to danger is 'flight' *from* danger *to* the mother, will the infant run *from* danger or run *to* mother? Is there a 'right' thing to do? Suppose it clings to mother. The more it clings, the more tense mother becomes; the more tense, the tighter she holds the baby; the tighter she holds the baby, the more frightened it gets; the more frightened, the more it clings.

This is how many people describe their experience of being unable to leave 'home', or the original other or nexus of persons in their life. They feel that their mother or family is smothering them. They are frightened and want to run away. But the more frightened they are, the more frightened and frightening their family becomes. They cling for security to what frightens them, like someone with a hand on a hot plate who presses his hand harder against it instead of drawing it away; or like someone who begins to step on a bus just when it begins to move away and 'instinctively' clutches the bus, the nearest and most dangerous object, although the 'sensible' thing to do is to let go.

One patient, Cathy, a girl of seventeen, was engrossed in a struggle to leave her parents. She could not do so in a real way, but developed a manic psychosis in which she 'left' her parents in a psychotic way by denying that her parents were her real parents. In a mental hospital, she ran away from the hospital repeatedly *in order to run home*, where she would arrive at any hour of the day or night and have to be dragged away again. For as soon as she got home she screeched and screamed that her parents were not letting her lead her own life, that they were dominating her in every possible way. Meanwhile the hospital was doing all it could to arrange for her to live away from home outside the hospital. The only reason she was in hospital was the disturbance she made when she got home.

She began to see me daily in hospital. Far from feeling that I might help her to gain her freedom, or to make use of the opportunities placed before her, she quickly began to attribute to me the same power-crazed drive to dominate and destroy her that she attributed to her parents. But she did not avoid me. On the contrary, in order to make her point she would follow me around shouting at me that I would not let her alone. A patient of Whitehorn (1958), while gripping his thumb in her fist as in a vice, shouted at him, 'Let go my hand, you brute.'

In the midst of her transference psychosis, Cathy dreamed: 'I am running as hard as I can away from the hospital, but the hospital, and you in it, is a gigantic magnet. The harder I try to run away, the more I am pulled towards it.' This phenomenon seems to be similar to some well-known hypnotic phenomena.

It may be that there is an instinctual 'tropism' to the mother which does not meet with an adequate terminating response in the mother. If Bowlby (1958) and others are correct, when an instinctual response system in the human being does not meet an appropriate terminating response in the other, then anxiety arises. If, however, the instinctual response to anxiety at some stage is to cling to the mother, then the more anxiety generated by the failure of an adequate terminating response in the mother, such as a highly 'confusing' reaction, a smile with tense facial muscles, soft arms, tight hands, and harsh voice, the more the 'need' for mother is stimulated.

There may be something wrong with the 'fit', with the interaction between mother and baby, so that within this context each starts to 'double-bind' the other. It is possible that an instinctual response is genetically set not to end itself, even when the terminating response is given, but goes on like a Sorcerer's Apprentice, unable to break its own spell. Prolonged intense clinging may begin to evoke 'double-bind-like' behaviour on the mother's part. Stimulated by it and exhausted, wanting the infant to continue and to give it up, she acts ambivalently. This in turn may contribute to the infant's developing a second level of disturbance, in that it may cease to respond to the mother at all, or begin to respond in simultaneously inconsistent ways, or in one stereotyped way. But speculation can go too far ahead of information. This field of research lies open, but curiously uncultivated except by a few.

CHAPTER 10

Attributions and Injunctions

THE attributes one ascribes to a person define him and put him in a particular position. By assigning him to a particular position, attributions 'put him in his place' and thus have in effect the force of injunctions.

Attributions made by Peter about Paul may be conjunctive or disjunctive with attributions made by Paul about Paul. A simple type of disjunctive attribution is: Peter makes a statement about Paul's relation to his testimony, with which Paul disagrees.

PETER: 'You are lying.'

PAUL: 'No, I'm telling the truth.'

Some attributions can be tested by consensual validation, but many things attributed by Paul to Peter cannot be tested by Peter, particularly when Peter is a child. Such are *global* attributions of the form 'You are worthless', 'You are good'. There is no way the recipient of such attributions *can* disconfirm them by himself, unless he controls the position[1] from which the person is empowered to arbitrate in such matters.

What others attribute to Peter implicitly or explicitly necessarily plays a decisive part in forming Peter's sense of his own agency, perceptions, motives, intentions: his identity.

Stephen lost all track of what his motives and intentions were, when for a period of his life he lived with a mother who had become 'paranoid'. She read motives and intentions into actions that he originally felt did not have such ascribed motives and intentions. Eventually his 'own' motives and

1. For a clever and by no means facetious study of psychoanalysis as a form of gamesmanship, see Haley (1958a). See also Haley (1958b).

intentions became entangled with those attributed to him. He knew if he cut his finger that his mother would say he had done so to upset her, and he, knowing that this would be her construction, could not be sure whether such was not indeed his intention. This engendered in him compulsive doubts about his 'motives' even for wearing a tie he liked, but which 'annoyed' his mother. 'You are wearing that to annoy me – you *know* I don't like ties like that.'

In the area of disjunction between the person's 'own' intentions and those attributed to him by other, issues of secrecy, deception of the other or deception of oneself, equivocation, lying, or telling the truth come into play. Much guilt and shame have to be understood in terms of such discrepancies, over such matters as being a fake, being a phoney. True guilt is guilt at the obligation one owes to oneself to be oneself, to actualize oneself. False guilt is guilt felt at not being what other people feel one ought to be or assume that one is.

It is an achievement to realize one is not necessarily who others take one to be. Such awareness of discrepancy between self-identity, being-for-oneself, and being-for-others, is painful. There is a strong tendency to feel guilt, anxiety, anger, or doubt if self-attributions are disjunctive with attributions made about self by other, particularly when attributions are taken as injunctions.

Joan's mother sent her a blouse for her twentieth birthday. The blouse had interesting characteristics. It was two sizes too big for Joan. It was not the sort of blouse she would have chosen for herself. It was very plain. It cost more than her mother could afford. It could not be changed in the shop in which it was purchased. One might expect Joan to be disappointed or angry. Instead, she felt ashamed and guilty. She did not know what to do with herself because *she* was not the right size for the blouse. She ought to have fitted the blouse not the blouse fit her. She ought to have been able to like it.

She ought to have fitted her mother's idea of who she was. In this case her mother confirmed the girl in the fact that she had a body with breasts, but did not endorse the actual body that she had. During puberty her mother had the habit of making remarks like: 'How are your titties coming along, dear?' Joan would feel her body going to pieces when her mother spoke to her like that. Presenting her with a sexless blouse too big for her was ambiguous and confusing. This girl was physically frozen and dared not be attractive and vital if her mother said in effect that she was not. The blouse, in being unattractive, implied an attribution: 'You are an unattractive young woman.' This attribution implied an injunction: 'Be unattractive.' At the same time she was mocked for being unattractive. Joan ended wearing the blouse, feeling helpless, despairing, and confused.

Attributions facilitate or undermine development or a feasible sense of self. Consider the following variations of a basic theme of childhood.

A little boy runs out of school to meet his mother.

1. He runs up to his mother and gives her a big hug. She hugs him back and says, 'You love your mummy?', and he gives her another hug.

2. He runs out of school; his mummy opens her arms to hug him, but he stands a little away. She says, 'Don't you love your mummy?' He says, 'No.' She says, 'Well, all right, let's go home.'

3. He runs out of school; his mother opens her arms to hug him and he stands away. She says, 'Don't you love your mummy?' He says, 'No.' She gives him a smack and says, 'Don't be cheeky.'

4. He runs out of school; his mother opens her arms to hug him and he stands a little way off. She says, 'Don't you love your mummy?' He says, 'No.' She says, 'But mummy knows you do, darling,' and gives him a big hug.

In (1), given no hidden ambiguities, there is mutual confirmation and conjunction. In (2) mother's invitation to the boy is turned down. Her question may be ambiguous, cajoling, and probing his feelings. She implies that he has feelings about her and he knows what they are, but that she does not know 'where she is' with him. He tells her that he does not love her. She does not dispute this and does not reject him. Will she 'leave him to get on with it' or 'let the matter drop?' Or find ways of punishing him or of having revenge, affect indifference, or seek ways to win him over to her, and so on? There may be some time before he will know where he stands with her.

In (3) the boy is treated as a separate being. His actions and testimony are not invalidated, but there are evidently rules governing when to say what. He is taught a lesson that it is sometimes better to be polite or dutiful than 'cheeky', even if cheeky is honest. He quickly knows where he stands. If the smack is not followed by other more complicated manoeuvres, the choice before him is clear cut. Watch what you say or you will be in trouble. He may know that, although his mother has smacked him for 'cheek', she is hurt and angry. He knows what he says makes a difference to her, and that if he hurts her she does not impose a burden of guilt by ambiguous appeals to remorse.

In (4) mother is *impervious* to what he says he feels, and counters by attributing feelings that overrule his own testimony. This form of attribution makes unreal feelings the 'victim' experiences as real. In this way real disjunction is abolished and a false conjunction created.

Examples of attribution of this order are:

'You are just saying that. I know you don't mean it.'

'You may think you feel like that, but I know you don't really.'

A father says to his son who was being bullied at school and had pleaded to leave: 'I know you don't really want to leave, because no son of mine is a coward.'

A person exposed to this type of attribution will have difficulty in knowing what his intentions or feelings are, unless he has firm ground under his feet. Otherwise he may no longer know when he feels one thing or the other, or how to define what he does.

Stephen's mother would blame him when *she* made a mess. She once came through from one room to another where he was sitting, and hit him. She had just broken a plate. Her reasoning appeared to be that she had broken the plate because she was worried about him, so he was worrying her, so he had caused her to break the plate.

When he was ill, his mother took some time to forgive him, because he was 'doing this', being ill, to upset her. Finally, almost anything he did was construed as an effort to drive her crazy. By adolescence he had no track of where his responsibilities, his effect, his influence, his power, began and ended.

What effect *can* one person have on another? Socrates remarked that no harm could be done to a good man. Hitler is reputed to have stated that he never deprived anyone of freedom, only of liberty. A prisoner in a cage could be supposed to retain his 'freedom', but to have lost his liberty. I can so act as to define the situation in which the other person has to act, but can I do more? If the other says, 'You are breaking my heart', am I in any sense 'doing' this to him? Jack acts in a particular way, and Jill says, 'You are driving me crazy.' It is everyone's experience that we act on each other. Where do we draw the line? By what criteria?

Jack is Jill's boy-friend. She goes out with Tom. Jack says that she is tormenting him. He is tormented 'by' her action, but she may not have gone out with Tom with any intention of tormenting Jack. If not, she could hardly be said to be tormenting him. But suppose that she did intend to torment him. Is she actually, in fact, tormenting him when (1) she intends to torment him and he is not tormented, (2) he is tormented when (3) she is not intending to torment him, and he is not tormented himself and (4) he is tormented. When Cordelia is invited by Lear to say to him the things she knows will make him feel happy, and she refuses, is she being cruel, if she knows he will feel hurt by what she says? In what sense do I do to the other what the other says I am doing to him, if I do what I want, with other intentions, knowing the 'effect' my action will have on him will be other than I intended, because *he* says so?

In many respects a child is taught what he is by being told what his actions 'mean', by their 'effect' on the others.

A boy of eight, who lived at home, had an older brother, much favoured by his parents, who was due to come home from public school for the vacation. The boy had repeated dreams of his brother being run over by a car or a lorry on his way from school. When he told his father this, he told the boy that this showed how much he loved his brother because he was concerned about his safety. He persistently attributed love of the older brother to the younger brother in the face of what to many would be indications to the contrary.

The younger brother 'believed' his father when he told him that he 'loved' his older brother.

Attribution works both ways. The child attributes good and bad, love and hate, to his parents, and conveys to them how he experiences them. What attributions do parents respond to, what are they impervious to, what do they accept or reject, what angers, flatters, or amuses them? What counter-attributions are provoked? 'Cheeky' is often the attribute for a child who attributes to his parents things they dislike.

Simultaneous contradictory attributions may carry concealed injunctions. When Margaret[2] was fourteen, her mother had two names for her, an old name 'Maggie' and a new one 'Margaret'. 'Maggie' meant she was still a little baby and always would be, who had to do what her mummy told her. 'Margaret' meant she was a big girl now and should be having boy-friends, not hanging about mother's apron-strings. One evening at six the girl was standing outside with some of her teen-age friends, her mother shouted from a window upstairs 'Margaret, come upstairs immediately.' This confused the girl. She felt everything draining from her and began to cry. She did not know what was expected of her. 'Margaret' was a grown-up, or at least an adolescent, role. It carried an injunction to behave independently. But the sentence following defined her as a little girl, 'Maggie'. As Maggie she was to do what she was told without thought or question. Everything drained from her as she had not the 'inner' resources to cope with being told to be Margaret and Maggie at once.

There are many ways of invalidating and undermining the acts of the other. They may be regarded as bad or mad actions, or they will be accepted in a sense not intended by the doer, and rejected in the sense actually intended. They may be treated as mere *re*-actions in the other to the person who is their 'true' or 'real' agent, as somehow a link in a cause-effect chain whose origin is not in the individual. Jack may be unable to perceive the otherness of Jill. He may expect credit or gratitude from Jill by making out that her very capacity to act is due to him. The more Jill does anything apparently freely, the more she is, as it were, operating by the grace and favour of Jack. If this happens between parents and children one finds the curious spiral: The more the child achieves, the more it has been given, the more it should be grateful.

Do not do what you are told. The person ordered to be spontaneous is in a false and untenable position. Jill tries to

2. I am indebted to Dr A. Esterson for supplying this example.

comply by doing what is expected of her. But she is accused of dishonesty for not doing what she really wants. If she says what she really wants, she is told she is warped or twisted, or that she does not know her own mind.

A successful professional painter was very slick at lifelike portraiture but could not bring herself to do abstracts. She remembered she used to make black messy drawings when she was a young child. Her mother, a painter herself, of insistently sweet flower arrangements and suchlike, valued 'free expression'. She never told her daughter not to make messes, but always told her, 'No, that's not *you*.' She felt awful inside when she heard this. She felt empty, ashamed, and angry. She subsequently learnt to paint and draw what she was told was 'her'. When she remembered the full force of her feelings about those early drawings which she had lost touch with without completely forgetting, she returned to her black messes after over thirty years. Only when she did could she fully realize how empty and twisted all her life had been. She felt what she called a 'cleansing shame' at betraying her own truest feelings. She contrasted this clean shame, in the strongest terms, with the 'shameful emptiness' she had felt when she had been told that these messy drawings were not really 'her'.

Some people undoubtedly have a remarkable aptitude for keeping the other tied in knots. There are those who excel in tying knots and those who excel in being tied in knots. Tyer and tied are often both unconscious of how it is done, or even that it is being done at all. It is striking how difficult it is for the parties concerned to see what is happening. We must remember that part of the knot is not to see that it is a knot.

Jill complains persistently that her husband, Jack, never let her 'have her own way'. He could not see why Jill felt exasperated, since he adopted the position that she could not do anything he did not want, since anything she did he wanted because he loved her.

The same arrangement of words, grunts or groans, smiles, frowns, or gestures can function in many possible ways according to context. But who 'defines' the context? The same form of words can be used as a plain statement of fact, as an accusation, as an injunction, as an attribution, a joke, a threat.

Jack says to Jill, 'It's a rainy day.' This statement could be intended in various ways:

1. Simply to register and share the fact that it is a rainy day.

2. Jack might have agreed reluctantly yesterday to go for a walk with Jill instead of going to see a film. By saying now that it's a rainy day he is saying, 'Thank God we will not be going for a walk. I'll probably get to see my film.'

3. Jack might be implying, 'Because it's rainy, I don't think you should go out'; or, 'Perhaps you do not want to go out (I hope) since it's raining'; or, 'I feel depressed. I don't want to go out, but if you insist, I suppose I shall have to.'

4. Jack and Jill might have had an argument yesterday about how the weather was going to turn out. The statement might mean therefore, 'You're right again', or, 'You see how I'm always correct.'

5. The window may be open. The statement may imply that Jack wishes Jill to close the window, etc.

Such multiple possible ambiguities are features of ordinary discourse. The above simple statement about 'the day' could imply a question, a reproach, an injunction, an attribution about self and other, etc. In 'straight' talk such ambiguities are present, but implications can be taken up by other which may in turn be admitted or, if not intended, can be honestly disclaimed. Frank and honest exchanges carry in them a great number of resonances, and the participants still 'know where they are' with each other. However, at the other end of a theoretical scale, conversations can be characterized by the presence of numerous disclaimed, unavowed, contradictory, and paradoxical implications, or 'insinuendoes'.

  (i) An ostensive statement is really an injunction.
     Ostensive statement: 'It's cold.'
     Injunction: 'Put on the fire.'
 (ii) An injunction is really an attribution.
     Injunction: 'Ask Jones for his advice on this.'
     Attribution: 'You are a bit of a fool.'
(iii) An offer to help is really a threat.
     Offer of help: 'We'll arrange a nice change for you.'
     Threat: 'If you don't stop behaving like this, we'll send you away.'
(iv) An expression of sympathy is really an accusation.
     Sympathetic statement (attribution): 'Your nerves are on edge.'
     Accusation: 'You are behaving atrociously.'

Jill may reply to each of the above statements by:
  (i) 'That's *really* an order.'
 (ii) 'You're really saying I'm a fool.'
(iii) 'You're really saying that, if I don't behave myself, you'll say I'm mad and get me put away.'
(iv) 'By saying you know I couldn't help myself, you find it necessary to avoid holding me responsible because you think I did harm.'

But Jack will deny that he has implied anything, and moreover imply that Jill is wrong, mad, or bad to think anything is implied. This implication in turn is made and disavowed. The next time a plain statement is made, and Jill reacts to it as a plain statement, she will be accused of being insensitive, or of wilfully refusing to 'know perfectly well' what is meant. Explicit levels may or may not be consonant with implicit levels, while on implicit levels the one person may convey two or more paradoxical implications at once.

Three or four persons in a closed nexus will maintain a *status quo* which suits them, forming a collusive alliance to neutralize anyone who threatens its stability. In such a family nexus, any statement or gesture functions as something quite different from what it 'appears' to be and no action can be 'trusted' to 'mean' what it seems. An outsider cannot discover what is 'really' going on for a long time. To an outsider, 'nothing' may be going on. Exchanges are boring, repetitious, concerned only with trivia. The energy of the nexus is used to prevent anything going on. One asks a child a question in the presence of her family. A 'sympathetic' aunt chips in, 'Tell the doctor what's upsetting you, dear.' The latent injunction is 'Don't comment. You are being told not to do or be what you are being told to do or be.'

'You are a bastard' may mean 'I dislike you, you are a nasty person, I am angry with you.' We tend to *assume* it carries such implications. Some people get into difficulties because they are never sure whether or not they are justified in making such assumptions. They earn different clinical diagnoses:

Is this a factual statement about my parents?
An attribution about me?
A statement about *my* feelings about you?
Serious or playful?

Many 'borderline' and schizophrenic patients are constantly puzzling over what is 'meant' by *any* statement, for any statement can function in innumerable ways. Was he being funny?

Was he telling me about my parents? Perhaps I should ask to see my birth certificate. Is he testing me to see if I'm 'touchy'? It is no longer constructive to see such preoccupations as 'ruminative thought disorder', and to seek the 'cause' in organic 'pathology'. The capacity to speak English is organically determined. So is the capacity to speak French, and the confusion of many bilingual children. Some people are taught several 'languages' in the same language. The difficulty that some persons have in 'knowing' or 'having the feel of' what 'language' or 'mode of communication' four words are in, may be due to having grown up in a nexus where black sometimes 'meant' black, and sometimes white, and sometimes both. Schizophrenic neologisms, amendments of syntax, queer intonation, splitting of words and syllables, and equivalent operations applied to non-verbal expression and gesture, require to be evaluated in terms of the system of communication in which they originally functioned, or continue to function.

The following are a few more glimpses of such interactions in families.

Mother, father, and patient (male, hospitalized paranoid schizophrenic of twenty) were arguing. The patient was maintaining that he was 'selfish', while his parents were telling him that he was not. The doctor asked the patient to give an example of what he meant by 'selfish'.

PATIENT: Well, when my mother sometimes makes me a big meal and I won't eat it if I don't feel like it.

Both his parents were silent. He had evidently carried his point.

FATHER: But he wasn't always like that, you know. He's always been a good boy.
MOTHER: That's his illness, isn't it, Doctor? He was never un-

grateful. He was always most polite and well brought up. We've done our best for him.

PATIENT: No, I've always been selfish and ungrateful. I've no self-respect.

FATHER: But you have.

PATIENT: I could have if you respected me. No one respects me. Everyone laughs at me. I'm the joke of the whole world. I'm the joker all right.

FATHER: But son, I respect you, because I respect a man who respects himself.

A boy of seven had been accused by his father of having stolen his pen. He vigorously protested his innocence but was not believed. Possibly to save him from being doubly punished as a thief and a liar, his mother told his father that he had confessed to her that he had stolen the pen. However, the boy still would not admit to the theft, and his father gave him a thrashing for stealing and for lying twice over. As both his parents treated him as though he both had done the deed and had confessed it, he began to think that he could remember having actually done it after all, and was not even sure whether or not he had in fact confessed. His mother later discovered that he had not in fact stolen the pen, and admitted this to the boy, without however telling his father. She said to the boy:

'Come and kiss your mummy and make it up.'

He felt in some way that to go and kiss his mother and make it up with her in the circumstances was somehow twisted. Yet the longing to go to her, embrace her, and be at one with her again was so strong as to be almost unendurable. Although he could not articulate the situation clearly, he stood his ground without moving towards her. She then said:

'Well, if you don't love your mummy I'll just have to go away,' and walked out of the room.

The room seemed to spin. The longing was unbearable, but suddenly, everything was different yet the same. He saw the room and himself for the first time. The longing to cling had gone. He had somehow broken into a new region. He was alone. Could this woman be connected to him? As a man, he thought this incident crucial in his life: a deliverance, but not without a price to pay.

There are endless ways in which a person can be trained to mistrust his own senses. To select only a few aspects for special comment, the injunction 'Come and kiss your mummy and make it up' seems to imply:

1. I am in the wrong.
2. I order you to make it up with me.

But it is ambiguous, for the injunction may be an entreaty masquerading as command. The mother may be pleading for forgiveness from the boy:

1. I did everything for your own good.
2. I appeal to you to make it up with me.

But the appeal, if it is an appeal, is backed up by 'blackmail'. 'I am still the stronger. If you don't kiss me, it does not matter all that much to me, and I will leave you.' The situation is hardly 'defined', rather there are innumerable flitting 'insinuendoes', multiple fractional implications. The person placed in a situation of this kind cannot make a meta-statement articulating any one of the multiple 'insinuendoes' without exposing himself to ridicule. Yet they are all there, and have a decisive cumulative effect. A few of these 'insinuendoes' are perhaps:

1. I am in the wrong.
2. I want to make it up with you.
3. Please make it up with me.
4. I order you to make it up with me.
5. After all, I did everything for your own good.
6. You ought to be more grateful for what I have done for you.
7. Don't think your father will believe you.

8. You and I know everything. No one else knows anything.

9. You know you need me. I don't need you.

10. If you keep this up, I shall leave you. That will teach you a lesson.

11. Well, there we are, it's all over now. Let's forget about the whole thing.

12. Mummy is not angry with you for all the worry she had over you and that silly pen.

13. Take it or leave it. If you leave it, I will leave you.
Equations may be:

to kiss me = to love me = to forgive me = to be good

not to kiss me = to hate me = not to forgive me = to be bad

The reader can easily construct a list of as many items again.

Betty's mother's favourite attribution about her was, 'She is very wise'. This meant that anything Betty actually did was very foolish, because in Betty's mother's view she never actually did the wise thing. Her mother persisted in believing that Betty knew what was 'the wise' thing to do, although by some peculiar aberration that could only be attributed to a 'mental illness' she always did the foolish thing. One of her favourite sayings was, 'She can do what she likes, of course, but I know that Betty is very wise and will always do the wise thing – that is, if she is well, of course.'

We have already considered Raskolnikov in *Crime and Punishment* from the point of view of his confusion of dream, phantasy, imagination, and waking perception. Dostoyevsky not only tells us this, but relates Raskolnikov's experience to the position he is 'placed' in before the murder. He displays Raskolnikov as 'placed' in a position that could be termed 'false', 'unfeasible', 'untenable', 'impossible'.

On the day before he murders the old pawnbroker woman, *a few hours before his 'terrible dream'*, Raskolnikov receives a letter from his mother. It is a long letter, about 4,500 words.

Its length contributes some of its essential qualities. As one reads it one comes to be enveloped in an emotional fog in which it is very difficult to retain one's bearings. When this letter was read to a group of eight psychiatrists, all testified to feelings of tension in themselves; two reported that they felt physically stifled; three reported that they felt marked visceral tensions. The quality of the letter that evokes this intense response is inevitably partially lost in the following extracts, but they enable some of the 'machinery' to become apparent.

The letter begins (pp. 48 et seq.):

My dear Roddy, ... it is over two months now since I had a good talk with you by letter, and I was so distressed about it that it kept me awake at night, thinking. But I know you won't blame me for my unavoidable silence. You know how much I love you, dear. You are all we have in the world, Dunya and I; you are our only hope of a better and brighter future. . .

She goes on to express concern about his career and their financial difficulties.

...But now, thank God, I think I shall be able to send you a little, and as a matter of fact we can congratulate ourselves on our good fortune now, which piece of good news I make haste to share with you. But first of all, my dear Roddy, I wonder if you know that your sister has been living with me for the last six weeks and we shall never part again. . .

We do not in fact discover what the good fortune is until about 2,000 words later, for Mrs Raskolnikov goes into a detailed account of her daughter Dunya's recent humiliation in the house of the Svidrigaylovs. She has not told Roddy before this because

If I had told you the whole truth, you would, I dare say, have thrown up everything and have come to us, even if you had to walk all the way; for I know your character and your feelings very well, and *I realize that you would never allow your sister to be humiliated.*

Dunya's character had been besmirched by Mrs Svidrigaylov, who had branded her as an immoral woman who was having an affair with her husband. However, Dunya was finally publicly vindicated, and

... everyone all of a sudden began to treat her with marked respect. All this was the chief reason for the quite unexpected turn of events, which I may say has completely changed our prospects. For I must tell you now, dear Roddy, that Dunya has received an offer of marriage, and that she has already given her consent, of which I now hasten to inform you. And though all this has been arranged without your advice, I am sure you will not be cross with me or your sister, for I hope you will agree that it was quite impossible for us to postpone Dunya's answer till we received a reply from you. And, besides, I don't expect you could have made up your mind without being present here yourself. It all happened like this ...

There follows a description of Dunya's fiancé, Peter Luzhin, 'a civil servant with the rank of a counsellor', which is a masterpiece of its kind.

... He is a distant relative of Mrs Svidrigaylov's, and it was indeed she who was chiefly instrumental in arranging the match. ... He had coffee with us, and the very next day we received a letter from him in which he very courteously asked for Dunya's hand in marriage and begged for a definite and speedy answer. He is a practical man and very busy, and he is now in a hurry to leave for Petersburg, so that every minute is precious to him. We were naturally very much surprised at first, for all this had happened very quickly and unexpectedly. We spent the whole of that day discussing the matter, wondering what was the best thing to do. He is a very safe and reliable man, has two official jobs, and already has money of his own. It is true he is forty-five years old, but he is fairly good-

looking, and I dare say women might still find him attractive. He is
altogether a highly respectable and dignified man, though perhaps
a little morose and overbearing. But quite possibly that is only the
first impression he makes on people. And, please, Roddy dear, I
must ask you not to judge him too hastily and too heatedly when
you meet him in Petersburg, which will probably be very soon, as I'm
afraid you're all too likely to do if something about him does not
appeal to you at the first glance. I'm saying this, dear, just in case,
for I'm quite sure that he will make a good impression on you.
And, besides, to get to know any man properly one must do it
gradually and carefully so as to avoid making a mistake and becoming prejudiced, for such mistakes and prejudices are very
difficult to overcome and put right afterwards. Mr Luzhin, to judge
by many signs, is a highly worthy gentleman. . . . There is of course
no special love either on her side or on his, but Dunya is a clever
girl and as noble-minded as an angel, and she will consider it her
duty to make her husband happy, and he, too, will probably do his
best to make her happy, at least we have no good reason to doubt
it, though I must say the whole thing has happened rather in a
hurry. Besides he is a very shrewd man, and he will of course
realize that the happier he makes Dunya, the happier his own
married life will be. As for a certain unevenness in his character,
certain odd habits, and even certain differences of opinion (which
can hardly be avoided in the happiest marriages) Dunya has told
herself that there is nothing to worry about. . . . He struck me at
first . . . as rather harsh, but after all, that is probably because he is
such an outspoken man, and indeed I am sure that is why.

The next section of the letter is dedicated mainly to con-
veying the idea that the only possible reason that Dunya is
marrying this obviously insufferably smug bore and tyrant is
for Roddy's sake.

. . . Dunya and I have already decided that even now you could
start on your career and regard your future as absolutely settled.
Oh, if only that were so! This would be of so great an advantage to
you that we must regard it as nothing less than a special sign of
God's grace to us. *Dunya can think of nothing else.*

Later:

... Dunya is thinking of nothing else now. During the last few days she seems to have been in a kind of fever, and she has already formed a whole plan about your becoming Mr Luzhin's assistant later, and even a partner in his legal business, particularly as you are studying law yourself.

Finally, she tells him that she and Dunya are coming to St Petersburg for Dunya's marriage, which 'for certain private reasons of his own' Luzhin wishes to get over as soon as possible.

... Oh, how happy I shall be to press you to my heart! Dunya is terribly excited and happy to be able to see you so soon, and she even told me once, as a joke, of course, that she'd gladly have married Luzhin for that alone. She is an angel!

The letter ends:

... And now, Roddy, my precious darling, let me embrace you till we meet again. Bless you, my darling! Love Dunya, Roddy. Love your sister. Love her as much as she loves you, and remember she loves you very much, much more than herself. She is an angel, and you, Roddy, are all we have in the world, our only hope of a better and brighter future. If only you are happy we shall be happy. Do you still say your prayers, Roddy, as you used to, and do you believe in the goodness and mercy of our Creator and our Redeemer? I am, in my heart, afraid that you may have succumbed to the influence of the modern spirit of godlessness. If so, then I pray for you. Remember, dear, how as a child, while your father was still with us, you used to lisp your prayers on my knees and how happy we all were then? Goodbye, or rather *au revoir*. Let me hold you close to me, my darling, and kiss you again and again.

Yours to the grave,

Pulcheria Raskolnikov.

Raskolnikov's immediate response to the letter is as follows:

Almost all the time he was reading the letter, from the very beginning, Raskolnikov's face was wet with tears; but when he had finished it, his face was pale and contorted, and a bitter, spiteful, evil smile played on his lips. He put his head on his old pillow and thought a long, long time. His heart was beating fast and his thoughts were in a whirl. At last he felt stifled and cramped in that yellow cubby-hole of his, which was more like a cupboard or a box than a room. His eyes and his thoughts craved for more space. He grabbed his hat and went out, without worrying this time whether he met anyone on the stairs or not; he forgot all about it. He walked in the direction of Vassilyevsky Island along Voznessensky Avenue, as though he were in a hurry to get there on some business, but, as usual, he walked without noticing where he was going, muttering and even talking aloud to himself, to the astonishment of the passers-by, many of whom thought he was drunk.

Let us consider the position that Raskolnikov is placed in by this letter. He is told: 'I realize that you would never allow your sister to be humiliated.' He is also told this his sister, after one frightfully humiliating experience, is in the process of undergoing what, as his mother makes clear to him, is an even greater humiliation. Whereas in the first instance she herself was b'ameless, in the second instance, by entering into a marriage that is no more than legalized prostitution, she is corrupting her own integrity. He is told that she is doing this only for his sake. And this he is expected to welcome.

But he has already been defined by his mother as a man who would never allow his sister to be humiliated. Is he at the same time to be a man who will allow her to sell herself for his sake? This is an untenable position.

Another twist to the tourniquet is turned around happiness. 'If only you are happy, we shall be happy.' In terms of the person he is supposed to be, how could he be made happy by such a state of affairs?

Yet another turn is added in respect of religion and godlessness. The whole concern of the major part of the letter is the sacrifice of one person's life, in order to provide enough money for another to get on in the world. This is taken as an index of Dunya's 'heart of gold', a suitably ambiguous expression, and of what an angel she is.

However, what is the position of a Christian placed in the position of being the recipient of this gratuity?

Dunya and her mother are only too glad to sacrifice themselves to invest in Roddy, 'our only hope for a better and brighter future'. On the one hand, they evidently wish him to make money in order to get them out of their rut. On the other hand, they tell him that all they want from him is his 'happiness'. Simultaneously, his mother fears that he may have succumbed to the 'modern spirit of godlessness' such as putting 'the world' before love!

To tease out all the strands in the entanglements of this letter, or even in the above extracts, the unavowed contradictions and paradoxes, the multi-levels of hypocrisy, would require an examination many times longer than the letter itself.

In reading the letter it is a useful exercise to imagine what would be the likely effect on the person for whom it is meant. As pointed out above, we must think transpersonally, not simply of the disturbance *in* the letter, but its disturb*ing* impact on another.

To summarize some aspects.

The person to whom it is addressed is placed in a non-compossible set of positions all at once.

There is a pervasive implicit injunction to collude at each of the multi-levels of hypocrisy; other attributions imply the impossibility of the addressee doing so; others in effect forbid him to be hypocritical, especially the final reference to the unspoiled religion of childhood, when the words are really believed for what they are.

He ought to be happy, because then 'we shall be happy'.

But being the man his mother tells him he is, he could never be so at his sister's great 'sacrifice'. Yet if he is not happy, he is making them unhappy. So presumably he will be selfish if he is happy, and selfish is he is unhappy and guilty to be happy, and guilty to be unhappy.

Dunya is repeatedly defined as an angel. 'Look what she is prepared to do for you', in effect. This carries an implicit negative injunction against daring to define her in a negative way, at the expense of being ungrateful. He would have to be a monster to have any feelings other than gratitude to such a heavenly creature, whose heart is eighteen carat, or to construe her action as any other than self-sacrifice. Yet if he is the man he is told he is, he must prevent it. Unless he does something awful, it is already *almost* a *fait accompli*. While being given grounds for hatred, resentment, bitterness, shame, guilt, humiliation, impotence, at the same time he is told that he should be happy. To move in any direction sanctioned by the letter, or to sustain consistently one position among the numerous incompatibilities *in* the letter, requires him to be defined within the framework of the letter as spiteful and evil.

He must not judge Luzhin too hastily or too heatedly when he meets him, 'as I'm afraid you're all too likely to do if something about him does not appeal to you at the first glance', although 'I'm quite sure that he will make a good impression on you.' The letter then proceeds to make it impossible that Luzhin could make anything but the worst possible impression on him.

He ought to be a Christian. But if he is a Christian, he would be evil to endorse such a godless plan for gaining money and social status in the world. He could endorse this plan if he were godless, but if he were godless he would be evil.

His thoughts in a whirl, stifled by the obligation to be grateful for this unsolicited sacrifice, he goes out, ruminating on how to stop Dunya marrying this awful man. Through their actions, his future is decided, unless he does something terrible, and this future is impossible.

The letter as it were explodes inside him. He is shattered, as one says. Dostoyevsky gives us some of the débris. Napoleon in imagination, a little boy in his dream, an old nag-woman in phantasy, a murderer in fact. Finally, through his crime and punishment, he wins through to Sonia, and Dunya finds happiness with his friend Razumihkin. His mother dies mad.

A Notation for Dyadic Perspectives[1]

ONLY if two people carry out reciprocally 'successful' acts of attribution can any genuine relationship between them begin.

Interpersonal life is conducted in a nexus of persons, in which each person is guessing, assuming, inferring, believing, trusting, or suspecting, generally being happy or tormented by his phantasy of the others' experience, motives, and intentions. And one has phantasies not only about what the other himself experiences and intends, but also about his phantasies about one's own experience and intentions, and about his phantasies about one's phantasies about his phantasies about one's experience, etc. There could be no greater mistake than to suppose that these issues are mere 'theoretical' complexities, of little practical relevance. There are some people who conduct their lives at several phantasy steps away from their own immediate experience or their own intentions. Family interactions are often dominated by these issues. An analyst or psychotherapist is constantly using his capacity to make, it is hoped, valid inferences about the patient's phantasies about him. The following is a short 'exercise' in this area, using a simple notation.

the own person, p
the way the own person sees himself, $p \to p$
the way the own person sees the other, $p \to o$

Similarly,

1. This schema has been developed in detail in Laing, Phillipson, and Lee (1966).

the other person, o

the way the other person sees himself, $o \rightarrow o$

the way the other person sees the own person, $o \rightarrow p$

the way the own person, p, views the other's, o's, view of himself, $p \rightarrow (o \rightarrow o)$

the way the own person, p, sees the other's, o's view of him, $p \rightarrow (o \rightarrow p)$

Similarly,

the way the other, o, sees the own person's, p's, way of seeing himself, $o \rightarrow (p \rightarrow p)$

the way the other, o, sees the own person's, p's, way of seeing him, $o \rightarrow (p \rightarrow o)$

$$> \text{ better than}$$
$$: \text{ compared to}$$
$$\equiv \text{ equivalent to}$$
$$\not\equiv \text{ not equivalent to}$$

The following are a few examples to illustrate the practical application of this shorthand.

Example 1

P's idea of o's idea of what he, p, thinks of himself, p

$$p \rightarrow (o \rightarrow (p \rightarrow p))$$

A little boy is being 'punished' for having done something 'wrong'. He does not feel sorry for what he has done, but knows that he is expected to say he is sorry and to look sorry.

What is involved for him at this point is:

$p \rightarrow p$ I'm not sorry.

$p \rightarrow (o \rightarrow p)$ Mummy is angry with me. She wants me to say I *am* sorry, and she wants me to feel that I *am* sorry. I know how to *look* sorry.

So that:

$$p \to p \not\equiv \qquad p \to (o \to (p \to p))$$

I'm not sorry.   She thinks that I am sorry
                        Therefore:
                        'I know how to take her in.'

This is based on $p \to (o \to (p \to p))$
the boy's idea that his mother sees him as sorry.
i.e. His idea is that she will feel something like, 'Now, he's a good boy again, he *is* sorry.'

But his mother may not be taken in.

She may see that it is 'put on' but let it pass.

She will have to mobilize the following degree of sophistication at this point:

$$o \to (p \to (o \to (p \to p)))$$

I see that he thinks I think he is sorry.

Example 2

P's idea of *o*'s idea of how *p* sees *o*.

$$p \to (o \to (p \to o))$$

e.g. A husband, *p*, thinks that his wife, *o*, thinks that he doesn't know that she does not love him any more.

This involves in general:

$$(p \to o)$$

his view of her.

The situation from the wife's, *o*'s, point of view would involve:

$$o \to (p \to o)$$

the way she thinks he sees her.

She might think:

$$o \rightarrow \qquad\qquad (p \rightarrow \qquad\qquad\qquad (o \rightarrow p))$$

'I suppose   he thinks   that I love him.'

From the husband's point of view:

$$p \rightarrow \qquad (o \rightarrow \qquad\qquad (p \rightarrow \qquad\qquad (o \rightarrow p)))$$

He thinks   his wife thinks   he supposes   she loves him.

Example 3

O has told a lie and has been found out. He is ashamed because he has been found out, not because he has told the lie $(o \rightarrow o)$.

p thinks o is ashamed of telling a lie:

$$p \rightarrow (o \rightarrow o)$$

o knows that p will 'melt' if he, p, thinks he, o, is ashamed:

$$o \rightarrow (p \rightarrow (o \rightarrow o))$$

so he acts as though he, o, thinks that p is still angry with him, o.

p thinks that o is acting this way because he, o, thinks that he, p, is still angry with him, o, because he, p, cannot understand how ashamed o is of himself, i.e.

$$p \rightarrow (o \rightarrow (p \rightarrow (o \rightarrow o)))$$

Example 4

$$o \rightarrow (p \rightarrow (o \rightarrow (p \rightarrow p)))$$
$$p \rightarrow (o \rightarrow (p \rightarrow (o \rightarrow p)))$$

e.g. A king and a court flatterer.

The king, p, wants someone to be frank and honest so that he can *really* know what the other thinks of him, i.e.

$$p \rightarrow (o \rightarrow p) \equiv o \rightarrow p$$

The other says, 'I can't flatter you', hoping that p will think that he, o, means this,

$$o \rightarrow (p \rightarrow (o \rightarrow p))$$

But p thinks, 'He thinks he can take me in with that old trick', i.e.

$$p \rightarrow (o \rightarrow (p \rightarrow (o \rightarrow p)))$$

Example 5

$$o \rightarrow (p \rightarrow (o \rightarrow (p \rightarrow o)))$$
$$\overline{p \rightarrow (o \rightarrow (p \rightarrow (o \rightarrow p \rightarrow o))))}$$

A 'paranoid' man, p

His wife, o

He is convinced that she is deceiving him in order to make him jealous; but he is not letting on that he knows this. So he pretends to be jealous (although he is not) in order to find out if it is true. But he is not sure that she may not be on to this.

i.e. He thinks she thinks that she has managed to trick him into being jealous, but she (i) may not be deceiving him, she might only be pretending to be deceiving him, so (ii) he will only pretend to be jealous, but (iii) she might be aware that he is aware that she is not sure whether he really is jealous. The estrangement from direct feedback can be seen perhaps better if the following 'onion' diagram is used.

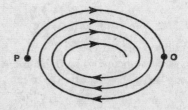

In this 'paranoid' position there appears to be a failure in negative feedback, and a sort of 'run away' into an almost infinite regress (obsessive-ruminative thinking, etc.).

We shall conclude these considerations by inviting the reader to ponder the skill of both parties in using attributions in this verbal fencing match between a husband and wife.

SHE: I love you, darling, you know I do.

$$p \to o \qquad o \to (p \to o)$$

HE: ... and I love you too, dear

$$o \to (p \to o) \equiv p \to o \equiv o \to (p \to o)$$

SHE: I love you, but you think I'm silly.

$$p \to o \not\equiv p \to (o \to p)$$

HE: That's projection

$$p \to (o \to p) \not\equiv o \to p \text{ but: } p \to (o \to p) \equiv p \to o$$
$$\text{or: } p \to p \equiv p \to (o \to p)$$

SHE: That's nonsense. You *do* think I'm silly.

$$o \to (o \to p) \not\equiv o \to p \quad p \to (o \to p) \equiv o \to p$$

HE: I never said anything of the kind.
   etc.

SHE: You just said I was.

HE: I said you were projecting.

SHE: That's what I'm saying; you don't respect me.

HE: That's not true, my dear, you *know* I respect you.

SHE: Don't tell *me* that I know you respect me. I know that you don't. You always think you know my own mind better than I know it myself.

HE: But you don't know your own mind. That's why you're seeing a doctor, and that's why you're ill. I am trying to help you; can't you see that?

SHE: You're not helping me a bit. You're trying to destroy me. You never could tolerate me thinking for myself.

HE: That's just what I want you to do. I'm not one of those husbands who think women should not be intelligent. I think you're a most intelligent woman.

SHE: Then why don't you treat me like one. I suppose you think that's what you were doing when you swore at me last night and called me a filthy bitch.

HE: I'm sorry; you made me lose my temper. You can behave abominably at times; that's just what you wanted me to call you. I forgot you were really ill.

SHE: I meant every word I said.

Finally the argument has the following structure:

p (the wife) says:.

$$p \rightarrow (o \rightarrow p) > o \rightarrow (o \rightarrow p)$$
$$p \rightarrow (p \rightarrow p) > o \rightarrow (p \rightarrow p)$$
$$p \rightarrow (p \rightarrow o) > o \rightarrow (p \rightarrow o)$$

o (the husband) says:

$$o \rightarrow (p \rightarrow p) > p \rightarrow (p \rightarrow p)$$
$$o \rightarrow (o \rightarrow p) > p \rightarrow (o \rightarrow p)$$
$$o \rightarrow (p \rightarrow o) > p \rightarrow (p \rightarrow o)$$

Selected Bibliography

*A number of works of immediate relevance to this study, to which no direct
reference is made in the text, are included below.*

ARENDT, H. (1958) *The Human Condition*. Chicago: The University
of Chicago Press.

BATESON, G., JACKSON, D. D., HALEY, J., and WEAKLAND, J.
(1956) 'Toward a Theory of Schizophrenia'. *Behavioral Science* **1**,
251.

BATESON, G. (1958) 'Cultural Problems Posed by a Study of
Schizophrenic Process'. In Auerbach (ed.), *Schizophrenia. An
Integrated Approach*. New York: Ronald Press.

BION, W. R. (1955) 'Group Dynamics: A Re-view'. In Klein, M.,
Heimann, P., and Money-Kyrle, R. E. (eds), *New Directions in
Psycho-Analysis*. Also in W. R. Bion, *Experiences in Groups and
Other Papers* (1961). London: Tavistock Publications; New York:
Basic Books.

BION, W. R. (1965) *Transformations*. London: Heinemann Medical
Books.

BINSWANGER, L. (1958) 'The Case of Ellen West'. Trans. Mendel,
W. M., and Lyons, J. In May, R. *et al.* (eds), *Existence – A
New Dimension in Psychiatry and Psychology*. New York: Basic
Books.

BOWLBY, J. (1958) 'The Nature of the Child's Tie to His Mother'.
Int. J. Psycho-Anal. **39**, 350.

BOWLBY, J. (1960) 'Separation Anxiety'. *Int. J. Psycho-Anal.* **41**, 89.

BRODEY, W. M. (1959) 'Some Family Operations and Schizophrenia'. *A.M.A. Arch. Gen. Psychiat.* **1**, 379.

BRONFENBRENNER, U. (1958) 'The Study of Identification
through Interpersonal Perception'. In Tagiuri, R., and Petrullo,
L. (eds), *Person Perception and Interpersonal Behavior*. California:
Stanford University Press.

BRUNER, J. S., SHAPIRO, D., and TAGIURI, R. (1958) 'Facial Features and Inference Processes in Interpersonal Perception'. In Tagiuri, R., and Petrullo, L. (eds), *Person Perception and Interpersonal Behavior*. California: Stanford University Press.

BRUNER, J. S., and TAGIURI, R. (1954) 'The Perception of People'. In Lindzey, G. (ed.), *Handbook of Social Psychology*, vol. 2. Cambridge, Mass.: Addison-Wesley.

BUBER, M. (1957a) 'Distance and Relation'. *Psychiatry* 20.

BUBER, M. (1957b) 'Elements of the Inter-Human Contact'. *Psychiatry* 20.

BURTT, E. A. (1955) *The Teachings of the Compassionate Buddha*. New York: Menor Books.

DOSTOYEVSKY, F. (1951) *Crime and Punishment*. Harmondsworth: Penguin Books.

DOSTOYEVSKY, F. (1958), *The Double. A Poem of St Petersburg*. London: The Harvill Press; Indiana: Indiana University Press.

FERENCZI, S. (1938) *Thalassa. A Theory of Genitality*. New York: The Psychoanalytic Quarterly, Inc.

FREUD, A. (1954) *The Ego and the Mechanisms of Defence*. London: Hogarth Press.

GENDLIN, T. E. (1962) *Experiencing and the Creation of Meaning*. New York: Free Press of Glencoe.

GENET, J. (1957a) *Our Lady of the Flowers*. Paris: The Olympia Press.

GENET, J. (1957b) *The Balcony*. London: Faber & Faber.

GIOVACCHINI, P. L. (1958) 'Mutual Adaptation in Various Object Relationships'. *Int. J. Psycho-Anal.* 39.

GLOVER, E. (1945) 'Examination of the Klein System of Child Psychology'. In *The Psychoanalytic Study of the Child*, vol. I. London: Imago.

GOLDSTEIN, K. (1957) 'The Smiling of the Infant and the Problem of Understanding the Other'. *J. Psychol.* 44, 175.

HALEY, J. (1958a) 'The Art of Psychoanalysis'. *ETC*.

HALEY, J. (1958b) 'An Interactional Explanation of Hypnosis'. *Amer. J. Clin. Hypnosis* 1, 41.

HALEY, J. (1959) 'An Interactional Description of Schizophrenia'. *Psychiatry* 22, 321.

HALEY, J. (1960) 'Observation of the Family of the Schizophrenic'. *Amer. J. Orthopsychiat.* **30**, 460.

HEGEL, G. W. F. (1949) *The Phenomenology of Mind* (revised second edn). London: Allen & Unwin.

HEIDEGGER, M. (1949) 'On the Essence of Truth'. In *Existence and Being*. London: Vision Press.

HEIDER, F. (1944) 'Social Perception and Phenomenal Causality'. *Psychol. Rev.* **51**, 358.

HEIDER, F. (1946) 'Attitudes and Cognitive Organization'. *J. Psychol.* **21**, 107.

HEIDER, F. (1958) *The Psychology of Interpersonal Relations*. New York: Wiley; London: Chapman & Hall.

HOPKINS, G. M. (1953) Gardner, W. H. (ed.), *Poems and Prose of Gerard Manley Hopkins*. Harmondsworth: Penguin Books.

ISAACS, S. (1952) 'The Nature and Function of Phantasy'. In Rivière, J. (ed.), *Developments in Psycho-Analysis*. London: Hogarth Press.

JACKSON, D. D. (1957) 'A note on the Importance of Trauma in the Genesis of Schizophrenia'. *Psychiatry* **20**, 181.

JACKSON, D. D. (1959) 'Family Interaction, Family Homeostasis and Some Implications for Conjoint Family Therapy'. In Masserman, J. (ed.), *Individual and Familial Dynamics*. New York: Grune & Stratton.

JACKSON, D. D. (1959) 'Schizophrenic Symptoms and Family Interaction'. *A.M.A. Arch. Gen. Psychiat.* **1**, 618.

JAQUES, E. (1955) 'Social Systems as Defence against Persecutory and Depressive Anxiety'. In Klein, M., Heimann, P., and Money-Kyrle, R. (eds), *New Directions in Psycho-Analysis*. London: Tavistock Publications.

JOURARD, S. M. (1968) *Disclosing Man to Himself*. New York: Van Nostrand.

LAING, R. D. (1960) *The Divided Self*. London: Tavistock Publications; (Penguins Books, 1965) New York: Pantheon.

LAING, R. D. (1965) 'Mystification, Confusion and Conflict'. In Boszormenyi-Nagy, I., and Framo, J. L. (eds), *Intensive Family Therapy*. New York: Harper & Row.

LAING, R. D. (1967) *The Politics of Experience and The Bird of*

Paradise. Harmondsworth: Penguin Books; New York: Pantheon.

LAING, R. D. (1967) 'Family and Individual Structure'. In Lomas, P., *The Predicament of the Family*. London: Hogarth Press.

LAING, R. D. (1969) *The Politics of the Family*. Toronto: CBC Publications.

LAING, R. D. and ESTERSON, A. (1958) 'The Collusive Function of Pairing in Analytic Groups'. *Brit. J. med. Psychol.* **31**, 117.

LAING, R. D. and ESTERSON, A. (1964) *Sanity, Madness, and the Family*. Vol. I. *Families of Schizophrenics*. London: Tavistock Publications; New York: Basic Books (1965).

LAING, R. D., PHILLIPSON, H., and LEE, A. R. (1966) *Interpersonal Perception – A Theory and a Method of Research*. London: Tavistock Publications; (Penguin Books, 1970) New York: Springer.

LAPLANCHE, J. and PONTALIS, J.-B. (1964) 'Fantasme originaire, fantasme des origines, origine du fantasme'. *Les Temps Modernes* **19**, 215. English translation: 'Fantasy and the Origins of Sexuality'. *Int. J. Psycho-Anal.* (1968), **49**, 1–18.

LEMERT, E. M. (1967) 'Paranoia and the Dynamics of Exclusion'. In Scheff, T. J. (ed.), *Mental Illness and Social Process*. New York: Harper & Row.

MINKOWSKI, E. (1933) *Le Temps Vécu*. Paris: Artrey, Coll. de l'évolution psychiatrique.

MOUNIER, E. (1952) *Personalism*. London: Routledge & Kegan Paul.

NEWCOMB, T. M. (1953) 'An Approach to the Study of Communicative Acts'. *Psychol. Rev.* **60**, 393.

NORMAN, R. D. (1953) 'The Interrelationship among Acceptance-Rejection, Self-Other Identity, Insight into Self and Realistic Perception of Others'. *J. Soc. Psychol.* **37**, 205.

PITTENGER, R. E., HOCKETT, C. F., and DANEHY, J. J. (1960) *The First Five Minutes*. New York: Paul Martineau.

RUESCH, J. (1958) 'The Tangential Response'. In Hoch and Zubin (eds.), *Psychopathology of Communication*. New York: Grune & Stratton.

SARTRE, JEAN-PAUL (1946) *The Flies (Les mouches)* and *In Camera (Huis clos)*. London: Hamish Hamilton; *No Exit (Huis clos)* and *The Flies (Les mouches)*. New York: Knopf (1947).

SARTRE, JEAN-PAUL (1952) *Saint Genet. Comédien et martyr*. Paris: Gallimard.

SARTRE, JEAN-PAUL (1957) *Being and Nothingness*. Trans. H. E. Barnes. London: Methuen.

SCHEFF, T. (1967) *Being Mentally Ill*. Chicago, Ill.: Aldine Books.

SEARLES, H. F. (1959) 'The Effort to Drive the Other Person Crazy – an Element in the Etiology and Psychotherapy of Schizophrenia'. *Brit. J. med. Psychol*. **32**, 1.

STRACHEY, A. (1941) 'A Note on the Use of the Word "Internal"'. *Int. J. Psycho-Anal*. **22**, 37.

TILLICH, P. (1952) *The Courage To Be*. London: Nisbet.

WATZLAWICK, P., BEAVIN, J. H., and JACKSON, D. D. (1967) *Pragmatics of Human Communication*. New York: Norton; London: Faber (1969).

WHITEHORN, J. C. (1958) 'Problems of Communication between Physicians and Schizophrenic Patients'. In Hoch and Zubin (eds), *Psychopathology of Communication*. New York: Grune & Stratton.

WINNICOTT, D. W. (1958) 'Transitional Objects and Transitional Phenomena'. In *Collected Papers*. London: Tavistock Publications.

WYNNE, L. C., RYCKOFF, I. M., DAY, J., and HIRSCH, S. (1958) 'Pseudo-mutuality in the Family Relations of Schizophrenics'. *Psychiatry* **21**, 205.

Index

Index

Klein, Melanie, 17n.

Laing, R. D., 36. 41, 50, 102, 137, 140
Laing, R. D., and Esterson, A., 41, 122–3, 134
Laing, R. D., Phillipson, H., and Lee, A. R., 174n.
Lemert, E. M., 134
Logical Type theory, 145, 148

Mann, Thomas, 129
masochism, 57
masturbation, 54–7, 59, 121
mechanism(s), 19, 21, 22, 26, 44, 57
melancholics, 52
memory, as mode of experience, 30, 32, 33
metapsychology, 25
Milne, A. A., 45
Minkowski, E., 135n., 137
mind, 24, 25–6, 129
motives, 27, 29, 95, 110, 151, 152, 174
Mounier, E., 37
mystification, 87, 140

Narcissus, 55
neurosis, 120
neurotic symptoms, 19
nexus, 41, 42, 43, 81, 86, 105, 136, 147, 148, 161, 162, 174
Nietzsche, F. W., 127
non-being, 51
nonentity, chaotic, 51

object(s)
  internal, 29 and n.
  transitional, 48, 49, 102, 105
ontogenesis, of confirmation and disconfirmation, 100

ontological insecurity, 50, 51
orgasm(s), 56, 85

pain, 33–4
Palo Alto group, 144–5, 148
paranoia, 151–2
  delusions, 132–3, 134, 138
  ideas of reference, 136
paranoid position, 179
parents, 86, 93–4, 95, 120, 137, 138, 144, 149, 162–3
penis, 57, 58, 59, 103, 104, 120, 131
perception, 29n., 30, 99, 151
personality, 19, 41, 139, 140
person as agent, 51, 101
person perception psychology, 29n.
phantasy(ies), 52, 53, 58–9, 68, 75, 86–7, 91, 93, 94, 110, 137, 138, 165, 174
  accounts of, 81
  acting out of, 61–8
  and communication, 33–43
  and experience, 17–32
  and orgasms, 55
  definition of, by Isaacs ,18–19
  destruction in, 84
  dread of, 93
  embodiment of, 48, 49, 57
  family systems of, 40, 41, 142
  group systems of, 42–3
  masturbation, 55–6
  nexus systems of, 42, 43
  shared systems of, 143
  social systems of, 38, 40, 41
  submergence in, 94
  terminology used by psycho-analysts in connection with, 23–4, 25
unconscious, 17ff., 94

REFERENCES TO CASES